FINE YACHT FINISHES

Paul and
Marya Butler

FINE YACHT FINISHES

FOR WOOD AND FIBERGLASS BOATS

INTERNATIONAL MARINE PUBLISHING COMPANY

Camden, Maine

Published by International Marine Publishing Co., a division of Highmark
Publishing Ltd., 21 Elm Street, Camden, Maine 04843.

Typeset by National Fisherman, Camden, Maine and Typeworks, Belfast, Maine.
Printed and bound by Rand McNally & Company, Taunton, Massachusetts.
Illustrations by Marya Butler.
Cynthia Bourgeault, Dennis Caprio, Barbara Hatch, Editors.
Janet Robbins, Production Coordinator.

Library of Congress Cataloging-in-Publication Data

Butler, Paul.
    Fine yacht finishes.

    Bibliography: p.
    Includes index.
        1. Yachts and yachting—Maintenance and repair.
2. Boats and boating—Painting.   I. Butler, Marya.
II. Title.
VM331.B86 1987   623.8'223'0288   87-3362
ISBN 0-87742-247-8

For JESSE,
of course

Contents

Preface

My first attempt at boat finishing was not auspicious. I was one of four eighth graders squeezing gobs of roofing tar into a gaping chine crack and slapping a hasty coat of skinned-over barn paint onto an old plywood cement-mixing trough that we had recently commissioned as an addition to our frogging fleet. I figured the big flat bottom would provide rock-solid stability on the pond, but I hadn't figured on spending most of my time with a bucket trying to keep the waterline somewhere below my knees. With a half-inch or so of crusted cement in the trough, it had long ago lost the usual advantage of positive flotation. It is still visible on a clear day when there's no breeze to ripple the water, 20 feet from shore and about eight feet under. Some 30 years later I'm still experimenting, and I only have to swim for it once in a while.

My real interest in finishing developed later, after a naively enthusiastic period of building small boats on my own, then a much-needed apprenticeship with a West Coast wooden-boat builder. I also did a lot of freelance boat maintenance, an intensive learning experience for an amateur, and as much sailing as I could manage. Although boatbuilding was the thing that really fired my imagination, I eventually figured out that no matter how fine a job you do of building, you have to protect and maintain that wood to get any long-term satisfaction. I never quite got used to the fact that most

boats are at their best when launched, and from that minute on they begin degrading. I still haven't accepted that premise.

After two years in the southern Philippines with the Peace Corps, trying to establish a vocational boatbuilding school on a tiny island in the Sulu region, I came back home, married a girl I had met earlier in California, and headed for the Northwest to build boats.

As a young girl, Marya lived with her family on a boat in the back bay of Newport Beach. With a strong background in advertising art and marine illustration, she soon honed her skills in freelance boat painting, varnishing, and gold-leaf work. She has the eye of a boatbuilder for a pleasing sheerline and can spot the tiniest glitch on a waterline; she has done the majority of the detail and finish work on all of our boats. Hers is the more delicate touch for that work, while I usually concentrate on preparation and setup.

Over the course of 20 years of boatbuilding, we have done strictly traditional plank-on-frame hulls and have found them, all things considered, to be the most fun to build but the most difficult to maintain. We have also done one-off fiberglass hulls over a male mold, production glass hulls using a female mold, and a number of cold-molded boats, ranging in size from 8 feet to 34 feet. We have worked at over a dozen boatyards from British Columbia to southern California, and we have done freelance finish and maintenance work and built motor and sailboats both on contract and on speculation. Many of our boats have been experiments in unusual rig, design, building, or finishing technique.

Even with this somewhat varied background, we admit to limited experience with many of the fine finishing products on the market. Finishers have a tendency to stick with those products that work for them instead of engaging in constant experimentation, which sometimes comes at a customer's expense. In addition, many boatyards and supply stores seem to stock only certain brands of paint, resin, varnish, brushes, sandpaper, etc. Small yards can't afford to carry a wide spectrum of the available products, so they tend to concentrate on those that are most often requested. We do not claim to be either impartial or omniscient; in sharing what has worked for us, we also reveal our blind spots and prejudices.

The area in which we probably differ from most finishers or builders is in our rather wide and varied use of epoxy. Building cold-molded boats, using layers of thin wood veneer and epoxy, led us to experiment with epoxy resins. Impressed with their remarkable versatility and efficiency, we have used them to solve a number of traditional boat maintenance and finishing problems. But like copolymer bottom paints and two-part paint, epoxy is not for everyone. It requires understanding and techniques to get the best out of it, and epoxy is often not the best treatment for traditional plank-on-frame hulls. It's ideal for cold-molded boats and has multiple uses for glass hulls and interior repair work, but it must be used with knowledge of its limitations. Those who prefer more traditional solutions to finishing problems will find plenty of them here.

Aside from our admitted bias toward epoxy, the other bias you will find is toward the possibility of a dedicated amateur bringing off a quality finish job. While it's true that certain sophisticated formulations, such as two-part polyurethanes, lend themselves to the sophisticated equipment and experience of a professional boatyard, even these fine finishes lie within the reach of a boatowner with a modicum of handiness and the appropriate mental attitude. The secret really lies in the mental attitude: a willingness to work carefully and methodically, to follow manufacturers' recommendations scrupulously, and to put in the time required for meticulous surface preparation. Given this attitude, the gap between professional finisher and dedicated amateur is a matter of experience, plus learning a few tricks of the trade. This book is here to bridge that gap.

Paul Butler
April 1987

Chapter One

First Things First

Preparation

The title of this book could just as easily be "Preparation and Finishing." Preparation is that 90 to 99 percent of the job done before you pry the lid off the can. Part of preparation could come under the heading of education. It's all the reading, sending away for literature, phone calls to the manufacturer, and other such groundwork essential to gaining competence and confidence. A little knowledge may be a dangerous thing, but a lack of knowledge is a guarantee of disaster. The other part of preparation, equally important, is the "hands on" kind; creating an adequate work environment, readying the intended surface — repair, sanding, filling, priming, more sanding, maybe more priming and filling — even selecting and cleaning the brushes beforehand and buying new mix pots.

With the variety of finishing materials currently available, preparation is more important than ever. High-tech finishes are by their very nature more sensitive to less-than-ideal conditions. It's no longer a matter of simply slapping on gobs of linseed with an old brush; these new finishes are very specific and effective formulations. They do a great job when applied according to instructions, but they flop miserably when preparation is neglected. Even products of lesser quality will usually do a decent job when matched with flawless preparation and application, while the best of products will fail without these things.

It's your first responsibility to start with undated, fresh materials when attempting important or critical jobs. You also should create a "window of opportunity," a time frame in which you can accomplish the project without undue interruptions. Visualize each move you'll have to make to complete the job, and plan for all contingencies. Have countermoves and foils prepared for weather, seagulls, jet aircraft traffic overhead, unexpected visitors, the cat — everything you can possibly imagine. The more complicated and demanding the project, the greater the importance of maintaining your concentration. Provide rags, solvent, drop cloths, and escape routes out of any corners into which you may paint yourself.

The work continues after the job is done. The surface must be watched and protected until the partially dry coating skins over and will no longer collect dust. Meanwhile, brushes must be cleaned, tools put away, and so on.

Before you begin, it may be wise to ask yourself a hard question: should I really be doing this project? Sometimes the honest answer is "no." There are times when each of us is too busy, too distracted, or just too extended to get involved in complex finishing projects. Disastrous results will affect more than just your pocketbook.

One important element in your decision

1

is the availability in your area of facilities qualified to do the work you have in mind. Delegating your project to a well-qualified yard may prove in the long run to be not only a blessing but an economy. A word of caution, however: the fact that a yard is *willing* to take on your work does not automatically guarantee that it is *competent* to do so. There are excellent yards with tenured employees who take pride in their work; these yards are usually financially sound and therefore often unwilling to take projects out of their areas of expertise. On the other hand, there are yards with ever-changing employees, who will take every job that comes their way as a matter of economic survival. Hiring such a yard to do the job may mean the work is done by a kid off the street making little more than minimum wage while the yard charges you $32 an hour for the privilege. Let the buyer beware!

Brands and Trade Names

When we began this book, Marya and I intended to include brand names we had worked with whenever relevant to the discussion at hand, and to provide a complete list of what is available in the marine marketplace. The list was to include products we had used, heard about, and researched as well as possible, but we realized that compiling a complete selection would be almost impossible. In addition to the diversity of products, we had to contend with a variety of opinion. There's an old saying in boatbuilding: Ask any three builders the same question and you'll get four different opinions. Another complicating factor is that geographical regions have favorite finishes that work well because of climatic and water conditions, and still another consideration is that we are biased according to our own experience. In the end, we thought it best to eliminate specific brand names from the body of the book in favor of generic descriptions. It pays to remember that specific products in most cases are not nearly as important as the care of preparation and ap-

plication. Nevertheless, because regional preferences do exist and are based upon accumulated experience, we have included an appendix to help you choose finishes that will work for you. It is not exhaustive by a long shot, but it is representative; we feel confident that if you use it as a guide you will buy brand names that are compatible with the climate to which your boat is subjected.

Most currently available products are good, few are really shoddy, and in most cases finishers can be assured that with a measure of common sense they will get through most finishing operations with a degree of success that will improve with experience. Almost all finishing operations are more successful the second time they are attempted, and as confidence increases.

Be aware of inflated, outlandish claims for products. Cure-alls, the snake oils and elixirs of the finishing trade, are scarce but do exist. A Sunday stroll through a marina and the asking of polite, interested questions will usually net enough information to help a confused beginner.

Faced with the prospect of using a new product every so often, we resort to our old habit of reading the labeling on the container and any literature we can obtain, scrutinizing in search of omissions as well as stated facts. The fine print on the side of the can is still the best source for each product. The manufacturer wants you to accomplish a successful job, wants your repeat business and your vocal sponsorship of its product. Manufacturers usually provide a phone number that will put you in touch with a qualified technical representative of that company who knows all about the product.

Levels of Workmanship

There are three general levels of workmanship, one of which the finisher will choose for each particular job, depending on the required result, the level of competence of the finisher, and the time and money available for the job. The first level is merely protective, or what is sometimes termed the "quick-and-dirty" finish job. This level requires some basic understanding of products and finishing methods, but it's not usually time-consuming. The quick-and-dirty approach requires a minimal amount of effort to accomplish the project, but it doesn't have to be sloppy.

The second level is fine finishing, perhaps the kind done by a talented professional concerned about time spent on the job. This level of finishing is usually sufficient for most boat owners and satisfying to all but the knowledgeable perfectionist. It is expensive if you have it done by someone else.

The third level is truly high-grade work, implying a quality of workmanship and materials not often seen. Usually only a skilled owner who can afford the time for preparation can accomplish such a result.

Safety With Finishing Products

The hazards involved in working with finishing materials are abundant, even with tradi-

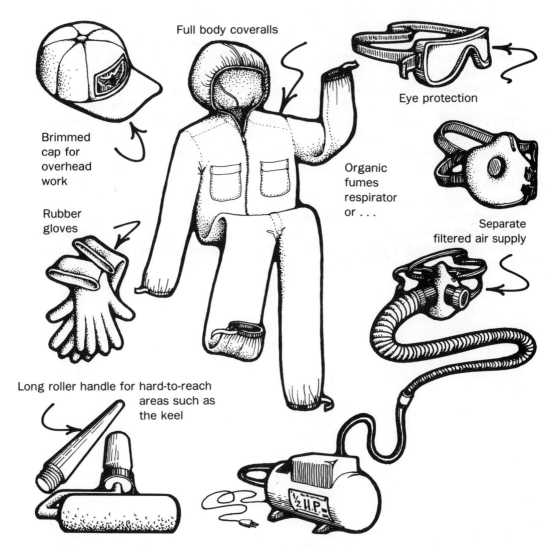

Full body coveralls

Eye protection

Brimmed cap for overhead work

Rubber gloves

Organic fumes respirator or . . .

Separate filtered air supply

Long roller handle for hard-to-reach areas such as the keel

½ H.P.

Working safely and cleanly is a must when dealing with today's highly toxic finishing materials.

tional materials, and seem to increase in potency as we use ever more powerful materials in the quest for longer-lasting, brighter, tougher paints and more poisonous, and therefore effective, bottom treatments. Unfortunately, the issue of safety and the all-too-often disastrous results of overexposure to these substances has not received adequate emphasis. After a while, those warnings on the can labels are taken for granted and ignored — until we actually get sick, by which time most of the damage may have been done. In most people, sensitivity to exposure builds slowly over a period of time, making the real problem difficult to detect. You notice that you're feeling nauseous or a little under the weather but attribute it to other causes, until the effects of prolonged overexposure manifest themselves in serious debilitating illness. We are not discussing merely dizziness or headaches that go away after a few days, but damage to neurological, respiratory, and cardiovascular systems. Serious stuff!

You can become sensitized to even the most docile of finishing materials, such as linseed, turpentine, and tung oil. In these cases, fortunately, prevention is quite simple: just wear gloves and provide plenty of ventilation when using these materials. But paints that are sprayed are potentially much more harmful, particularly those with strong solvents; most require positive pressure respirators with separate air supplies. When using these materials, you need far more than the traditional dust mask and a modicum of ventilation. Even the organic fumes mask alone is insufficient.

The cautions to avoid breathing the fumes and to avoid skin contact extend to virtually the entire range of finishing materials. Acetone, for example, can be absorbed into the skin and do serious nerve damage. Two-part cleaners contain lye and acids; paint strippers contain methanol and ethanol and ketones. The list goes on to include fluorides, phenols, lead, zinc chromates, and other powerful, harmful (and frankly scary) materials. Two-part urethane topside paints and the copolymer bottom paints, those relatively new products that do such an effective job, contain cyanides in the form of isocyanates. These are among the most dangerous of finishing materials and should never be allowed to contact the skin. This means full body protection and positive pressure respirators.

The bottom line is that prevention is relatively inexpensive compared to the consequences of ignoring the warnings. In fact, it's downright cheap. Educate yourself about the products, and arm yourself with a measure of good sense and a healthy dose of caution.

Chapter Two

Brushes

Bristle Types and Conditions

Quality brushes may be hard to locate in areas that do not sustain a regular demand from finishers. Sometimes a small paint store will stock only one brand or type of quality brush and in such cases you will be encouraged to buy that brush, whereas in a mail order catalog, you can shop the entire line. If you wish to learn more before you buy, go to a paint or finishing products store and ask if you can have a few of their old trade magazines. They contain a wealth of information, addresses of brush manufacturers and often a toll-free telephone number for more information.

The bristle of a quality brush is packed tightly at the ferrule and tapers gradually to the tip. The bristle is held securely in place, usually set in rubber or epoxy. In quality brushes, the bristle is usually packed in various sorted lengths from the ferrule to support and provide a livelier action to the tip of the brush. Most better brushes have small wedges inserted inside the ferrule, and the space resulting from the wedge or wedges

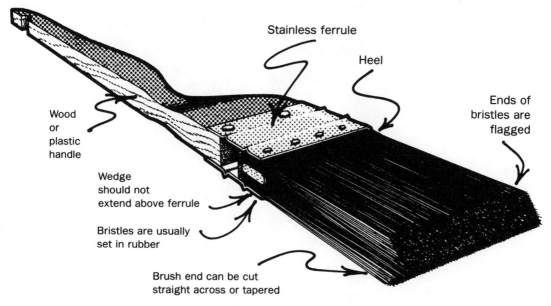

Stainless ferrule

Heel

Ends of bristles are flagged

Wood or plastic handle

Wedge should not extend above ferrule

Bristles are usually set in rubber

Brush end can be cut straight across or tapered

Cross section of a typical brush.

inside the ferrule forms small pockets that hold a bit more paint or varnish. These pockets extend the range of each brush stroke. Whether the wedges are there to provide the air space or to save on the amount of bristle used in each brush, they seem to work. Some older brushes had no wedges at all, just tightly packed bristle.

Natural Bristle

Bristle type and quality is the single most important component of a fine brush. Badger bristle was at one time considered top of the line for fine finish work. It is still widely available on special order, but most natural bristle brushes sold in this country today are made of hog bristle, otherwise known as Chinese or China bristle because much of it is imported from China. It makes a reasonably priced quality brush that will produce a good finish.

Chinese bristle is sorted into a variety of grades and colors and often mixed with other bristle types to achieve specific characteristics. One catalog, for example, lists an ox hair/Chinese bristle for topsides and varnish application. The ox hair provides a more delicate touch. The same catalog has a brush of mixed Chinese bristle and polyester for bottom paint applications.

There's a mystique among finishers surrounding the use of exotic-bristle brushes and their ability to improve the quality of work. Quite possibly in the hands of expert finishers of vast experience they make a substantial difference, but we know of several professional finishers who prefer a good Chinese bristle, or a blend of bristle and synthetic filament, over the badger bristle brush. The important factors in successful combinations are probably due mostly to experience rather than exotic bristle.

Natural bristle is flagged. This means quite simply that the tip ends of the bristle are split, something that happens naturally to grown bristle. Your own hair probably

Flagged bristle.

does it, and in the case of fine brushes, it's an advantage. The split ends lift and carry more paint or varnish and let it down onto the surface with a smoother, more controlled action than unflagged bristle. Try an experiment with a small nylon bristle brush and a flagged bristle. Dip them in oil or paint and apply it to a surface; you will immediately understand the difference in control. Varnish or paint runs right off straight bristle, but the flagged tips hold it and release it as you pull the brush across a surface. The flow is much smoother and more uniform. A close look at a brush with flagged bristle will show that probably more than half are flagged, and this is apparently sufficient.

Natural bristle is also tapered from the heel of the brush to the tip, just as it grows on the animal. This taper provides a firmer support for the bristle as it comes out of the ferrule, while it allows the necessary flexibility and resilience down near the tip. Taper supports the delicate flagged ends of the bristle as they apply the finish, plus it aids the smooth flow of paint or varnish down onto the tip of the brush.

Chinese bristle can be either black or white or brown or any color you can grow a pig, and contrary to what some finishers believe, the color has little bearing on the quality of the brush. The best brushes are not necessarily solid white, or solid black, for example. The quality of the bristle is what matters; the taper, flagged ends, and flexibility of the bristle make the difference. Bristle is sometimes dyed black, but this has little to do with performance.

Natural bristle has oils that protect and give the brush longer life. Water-based paints and hot solvents attack and remove the natural oils, and eventually ruin a brush for use in fine finishing. For this reason, many professionals recommend treating natural bristle with oils to improve characteristics and prolong useful life. You can make a workable brush oil solution from linseed oil thinned slightly with kerosene; an occasional short soak will help maintain the natural bristle. A friend of ours uses a 10W40 motor oil; obviously, the brushes will need a cleaning before use.

Synthetics

Brushes made of manufactured bristle, usually called filament, will do a creditable job and may be used with all types of finishes. Chinese bristles may also be used for all types of finishing, including water-based paints and industrial finishes, such as two-part polyurethane, but synthetics are often chosen for these jobs because they offer more durability and resistance to strong solvents, and they hold their shape better than natural bristle. Water-based paints in particular are very hard on a quality Chinese bristle brush. Many professionals now use synthetics because they're less expensive, more available, durable, and effective.

Synthetics already come very close to duplicating the action of a grown bristle. There are solid- and hollow-tapered synthetic bristle, and the solid-tapered type probably best simulates the premier action of natural bristle. A close look at a synthetic brush and a comparison of available types will provide the best information to a prospective buyer. Hold the brush in your hand and fan the filaments. Make sure they are well anchored in the ferrule. If you can easily pull pieces of filament from the ferrule, the brush obviously isn't going to last very long when soaked with paint and cleaning solutions. Good synthetic bristle is flagged like natural bristle, so check for this if you're looking for a quality synthetic. The tip should be trimmed like a Chinese bristle brush, flat across for sash and trim brushes, and with a slight bevel or oval tip shape for other types.

The two common types of synthetic filament are polyester and nylon. These are also used in combination with each other and with Chinese bristles for certain characteristics. Sometimes you find inexpensive imported brushes made of polypropylene, but they look like brooms and probably work as well. Nylon wears the best and will apply paint with a softer and more sensitive touch. But nylon will also absorb small amounts of water, and if you're using water-based paints the filaments may become softer and more limp as you paint.

Polyester filaments are tougher than

nylon and stand up to water-based paints much better. They perform much better in very hot or very cold conditions because they hold their shape and flexibility much better than nylon. Polyester filament is also more resistant than nylon to strong solvents, which explains why a blend of these types is so good.

A good synthetic brush will outlast many times over a brush made of natural bristle, probably at least six to one, so if you're concerned about getting the maximum use from your brush, synthetics are strong contenders. When you shop for these types, look for a quality synthetic; locating the best may take some time. All synthetics are cleaned using the same techniques as for Chinese bristle brushes.

"Blow-out"

If the bristles tend to separate from each other and refuse to lie together, they are "blown out." A brush with blow-out will be difficult to use; it will not leave a clean cutting-in line and will not apply a smooth finish because those random strands of bristle drag paint to each side. A stray bristle also ruins my concentration because I tend to watch it continually. Many quality brushes may show the characteristics of blow-out when they are air dried without a proper cleaning, but when you wet them, they will once again assume the proper lay and profile. Any water-based paint is very hard on natural bristle and will eventually cause a bad case of blow-out.

A brush should be cleaned, then combed with a bristle brush before dry storage to avoid this problem. If you don't have a bristle brush, any comb will work. A good brush should also be wrapped to keep the bristle together during long-term storage.

Blow-out in an older brush may be a sign that the brush is wearing, or that it has been improperly used. Using a flat brush for trim work by holding it sideways also will eventually cause blow-out. Keep a small brush especially for trim jobs, or get a tapered trim brush. If the bristle refuses to lie in proper profile, even after careful cleaning, bristle brushing, and wet-out, a last resort to get a bit more work out of the brush is to try to trim off the errant bristle. Almost all cheaper brushes display blow-out and splayed bristle pattern at the end, sometimes even when they are brand new, and this means they're useless for fine finish work.

"Fingering"

Fingering is the separation of bristle and filaments into clumps of "fingers." It's caused by improper cleaning, such as soaking too long in solvent or water-based paint, or using a wire brush to strip out dried paint from the heel. It can also be caused by improper use, such as painting a 2-inch rail with a 4-inch brush; holding the brush on edge instead of flat; or stippling instead of pulling across the surface.

If you're working on a large project, it's a good idea to stop during the day and clean the brush at least once, maybe more in warm weather. A good cleaning and a bristle combing may remedy the fingering if the brush is still salvageable.

Brush Preparation and Maintenance

Fine-tuning and cleaning are as important as choosing the right brush in the first place,

Blow-out.

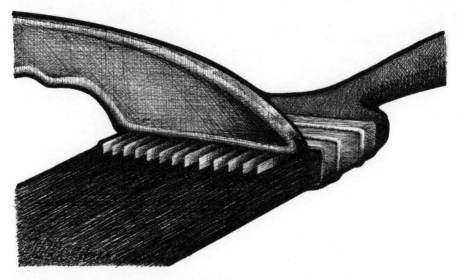

Brushing with a hair comb or bristle comb keeps bristles straight. Comb brush after cleaning. Allow to dry.

and even the finest-quality brushes need some conditioning to achieve best results when they are new. Good brushes will eventually become old friends, but first you have to work with them and develop confidence in their ability.

Before using a new brush you should remove dust and any loose bristle, paying particular attention to the heel and under the ferrule where short pieces of bristle hide. New brushes must always be cleaned before using because bristle and filament are often stacked in a brush — shorter lengths up closer to the ferrule — and unattached pieces may be hiding in the brush. A bristle comb sometimes helps get into the body of the brush and is probably necessary if you're doing a delicate varnish job. Hold the brush in one hand and twirl the bristle over the palm of the other hand. You also might want to fan it over a vaccum nozzle.

Bristle Trim

Fine brushes always come with a near-perfect trim to the bristle tips, and usually not until they are much used, or abused, do they develop an improper "footprint" and require retrimming. If the brush eventually fails to give a smooth flow of paint or var-

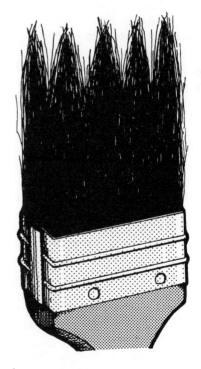

Fingering.

When preparing for a fine finish job, fan the brush over a vacuum nozzle to collect remaining dust and any loose bristle.

nish across the length of the tip, it may be telling you that trimming is needed. Cheaper brushes may need a trim right away to produce the desired effect; experience is important in knowing, and it's good to have a quality brush with which to compare. A close look at the tip of a good brush will show a workable profile.

Sash brushes used for cutting in and painting narrow moldings seem to work best with a slight flat on the tip, but most other brushes work best with a slight oval-trimmed tip. In use the brush is flexed slightly to one side or the other, and in this flexed position it must present the proper footprint to the surface. You can make a fine sash brush from an old worn straight brush simply by trimming the tip to an angle of 30 degrees, or thereabouts.

Reasonable care in trimming a bristle will usually produce a serviceable brush. Cutting with a sharp pair of scissors is one way, and trimming with a new single-edge razor blade also works if the bristle is supported on a cutting board.

One method for trimming is as follows: Separate the brush into equal halves by slipping a thin piece of plywood between the two halves and up against the ferrule. Trim each side separately with a new single-edged razor blade, tapering each side toward the middle.

Match the two sides as carefully as possible, recutting if one side is longer than the other. After the thin plywood is removed, finish the job with sharp manicure scissors, cutting a small flat on the tip. To encourage splitting or flagging of the bristle, swat the tip a few times across a plank edge. Some finishers trim brushes very successfully with everything from tin snips to a sharp jack knife. Best to experiment and use whatever works for you.

Brush Cleaning and Storage

Any brush, whether of excellent or poor quality, can be used only a dozen or so times before the heel, which can never really be perfectly cleaned, accumulates paint or varnish and starts letting it down onto the work. Capillary action will draw paint right up into the tightly packed bristle inside the ferrule, small bits of which will be impossible to remove and will eventually harden. When this happens, the brush must be retired from front line duty, on your most exacting finishing work, although it may continue to have a useful life in less demanding jobs. Any brush used regularly will last only so long even under the best of conditions.

Proper and regular cleaning is, however,

A sharp blade trims bristle ends.

the solution to most of the routine problems that good brushes suffer, and thorough cleaning is the only way to realize a full life from a brush. Problems will sneak up after a period of bad maintenance and catch you unaware; suddenly you will be dealing with errant bristle that strays in every direction, a brush that's impossible to keep clean during a job, and other small problems that detract from good finishing.

Once a brush has been used for paint, it will be hard to get a good varnish job from it because small bits of paint in the heel will be dissolved by the varnish and let down. You may get away with it for a very quick small job, but for larger jobs you will be surprised by the various tints to your varnish. For this reason most finishers keep a brush *just* for varnish, and also a brush *just* for white.

Synthetic filament is usually more difficult to clean than natural bristle. Since synthetic bristle is most often used when working with water-based paints, which dry more quickly than other types, these brushes require more soapy washes and rinsing. Stubborn cleaning jobs on synthetics used with oil-based paints may call for a bath in paint thinner to aid cleaning, followed always with a soapy wash and thorough rinse. The solvents used in two-part polyurethane paint are also quite harsh and deteriorate a brush sooner than normal wear, and once two-part paint hardens in the heel of the brush it will be almost impossible to remove. It's always wise and produces a better job to use one set of synthetic brushes for oil-based paints and another set for water-based paints.

Some companies market a liquid brush cleaner, and you may want to try one for obstinate cleaning jobs, but after immersion in the cleaner the brush should be shampooed in a mild solution of soap and water. Rinse well, then comb to remove curls or twists and replace in the storage envelope.

A typical brush-cleaning method might go as follows: Strip out as much of the paint or varnish residue as possible by running the brush carefully over an edge and/or on a plank, and then by twirling and wiping it on a rag. This should be done carefully and efficiently so as not to confuse the bristle more than necessary. The next step is to use solvent to get more residue out, paying particular attention to the heel of the brush. Then, using a can or jar that fits the size of the brush fairly well, suspend the brush in the cleaning solution, just enough to cover the bristle and part of the ferrule (see illustration, p. 14). You may wish to soak it overnight, but longer soaking can harm the brush. Swish the solvent around when you immerse the brush to release any air bubbles trapped in the ferrule. Later on the same day (or the following day) slosh the brush around, shake out the solvent, and use the same jar to soak the brush again in a strong soapy solution. After this second soak, slosh the brush well, rinse for about ten minutes, wrap the bristle in a paper towel, and tape the paper in place. Squeeze the paper-wrapped bristles carefully in a vise if you have one handy and hang the brush to dry, first making sure that the bristle is neat. If the bristle is wild, comb it again to straighten. If your brush came with one of those snap-on folded envelopes, it's best to use that for storage because it will hold the bristle securely. For the best results, put the brush in the envelope before the brush is completely dry.

Soaking as a brush-cleaning technique should be used with care. Soaking for long periods in plain water is particularly harmful to fine natural bristle brushes. It eventually causes handles to crack, ferrules to rust, and bristle to become limp and lifeless. A fine natural bristle may never recover from long-term soaking. Overnight soaking in a mild solvent is the most that should be allowed, and the best policy is to clean the brush right after the job if possible. If you're in the midst of a large job that takes several days, however, it may simply be too much bother to clean and dry a brush every night. Some painters use a kerosene rinse, or kerosene with a little motor oil added as an overnight solution, but the brush must be rinsed in clear thinner before use the next morning.

When you strip paint or varnish from a brush, don't hammer the ferrule edge on a rock or the edge of a plank. This hammering will indent and bend the ferrule and may cause chunks of the bristle to break loose from the setting. Brushes with a flexible bristle setting are least likely to break, but hammering is a poor technique for cleaning excess residue from a brush. Spinning or shaking is a better method for stripping the brush in preparation for cleaning, and brush spinners are available to do the job without harm to the brush.

A good brush with bent bristle or filament as a result of improper storage or cleaning can sometimes be salvaged by a dip in very hot water, a thorough bristle combing, and a proper air dry. You may have to repeat the process until all the shape is out of the bristle. Don't leave the brush to cook in hot water; a dip of a minute or less is entirely adequate. A brush comb may help restore shape to the bristle during this process. If the brush has been left to dry without cleaning, restoring it to good condition may be impossible.

Certain solvents for brush cleaning, including common paint thinner, may be used over and over again by allowing the cleaning

can to settle and then pouring the clear solution off the top. You can save about 80 percent of each batch of cleaning solvent. We work with two or three cans, rotating them as each becomes dirty. After cleaning your brush, seal the solvent in a lidded coffee can and set it aside for a few days. Open it carefully, and the sediment will have separated out, leaving the clean solvent on top. Pour that carefully, so you don't disturb the bottom, into another container for reuse.

After you've cleaned your brushes, you have to have a place to store them. Just a corner of a locker with a few hooks or a clean drawer will do. All you really have to do to maintain a brush is to clean it, air-dry it, and wrap the bristle. It's always better to hang a clean brush, but wrapped in the stiff storage envelope it can be laid in a drawer with other brushes with no harm at all.

If you have a number of quality brushes and you use them for a variety of finishes, mark and separate them according to the finishes for which they are used. Varnish brushes, for instance, should be kept exclusively for varnish until they stop performing well, at which time they should be relegated to the compartment containing paint brushes or the second-string brushes. By maintaining a stockpile of slightly worn veterans, you have brushes suitable for primers, oiling, bottom paint, and other less demanding applications.

Drill holes through the handles of all your good brushes, which will make them easier to store and will also allow you to stick a stiff wire or wood dowel through the handle to suspend the brush in a can filled with cleaning solution. Most brushes come with one small hole in the end of the handle, but you may wish to drill another larger hole down closer to the ferrule, which will give a depth adjustment option when you hang the brush for cleaning.

Brushing Technique

While a quality brush will obviously improve your ability to create a fine varnished or

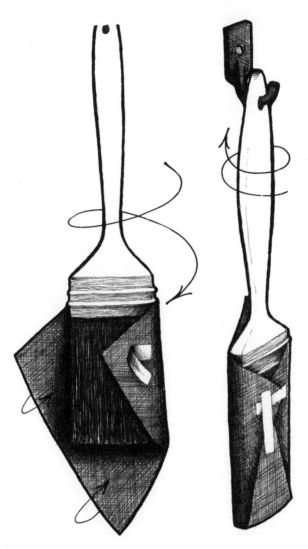

After a brush has been cleaned and combed, wrap it in stiff paper. Store a brush either by laying it flat or hanging it up.

painted surface, almost any clean and controllable brush of the proper size will do for small jobs and quick touchups. If the brush will quickly and evenly spread the varnish, without major sags and without leaving bristle pieces in the varnish, then within four or five minutes most any bubbles and other small imperfections caused by uneven flow of varnish onto the surface will self-level and disappear. Any particularly stubborn bubbles that persist, sometimes caused by working in cold weather or with cold varnish, may need to be removed by flipping them with the edge of the brush. Proper thinning, if re-

quired, and speed are sometimes more important with certain small jobs than a high-quality, fine-tuned brush. If you have to get a patch of exposed bare wood covered before the evening fog bank covers the marina, or if you want to do a quick touchup to a recently scraped section of footrail before you leave, it's far more important to get the varnish applied than to worry about minor details, which can often be dealt with later. For such jobs the varnish should be applied and left alone, not pestered with the brush. Cheap and disposable foam brushes will quite often do a good job in these cir-

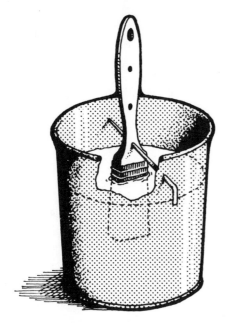

Drilling additional holes in the handle allows the brush to be adjusted to the depth of the solvent during a soak.

nish on new wood, many finishers prefer to lay on the varnish across the grain, then come back and smooth the varnish with the grain to get a uniform coating on the wood. Load the brush for the cross-grain stroke and then go with the grain using a dry brush. By the time you have three or four coats on the wood, it's no longer necessary to stroke across the grain, and you can take long even strokes in the easiest direction, usually longitudinal for rails and moldings and horizontal for large vertical or flat areas.

Start at the top and work down across a large transom or topsides. For best control and concentration, get all the scaffold work done at the onset of the job and finish by standing on the ground.

Overlap your brush strokes. A brush will usually leave a mark where you put it down, but not where you pick it up, at least not if you're careful and lift it off with a swinging motion, twisting the brush slightly as you do so. The description seems more complicated than the procedure, and it becomes second nature with a little practice.

Finish a section before starting another, if you can. When some finishers work on a large area, they make an X across the surface and paint in that area before moving to another spot. If you can, make one complete brush stroke all the way across a section, but if the piece is too big, plan an overlapping motion to cover where you begin and end a brush stroke.

cumstances. They're not for large areas or fine work, but they do the job and you can forget the time-consuming process of brush cleaning. You can buy these brushes for less than the cost of materials to clean a fine brush.

Brush strokes should be light and positive. Pull the brush across the wood; don't stipple or poke the bristle onto the grain of the wood. For the first coats of var-

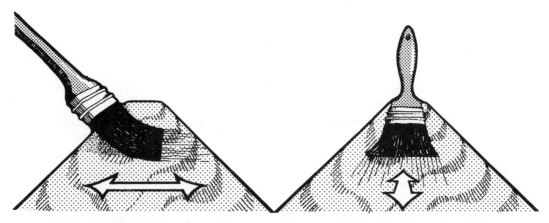

Apply the first coats of varnish across the grain (left), then come back and smooth with the grain (right).

A slight twist of the brush will mark the lift-off and start of overlap for the next stroke.

On a long, hot day when the paint dries quickly, your brush may start to harden while you're working. Thinners evaporate, and the pigment drawn up into the bristle begins to harden. Bristle sticks, begins to separate into fingers, and makes a good clean stroke more and more difficult. The solution to this problem is to work with two brushes, and halfway through the job, or when necessary, suspend the first brush in cleaning solution while you start fresh with the second brush. Unless you have someone to clean your brush while you work, suspend the bristle in a cleaning solution rather than throwing it in a can or jar.

You'll quickly see that when you varnish around hardware or over a sharp edge, it's very difficult to avoid leaving a drip or a run if you have a loaded brush. Every finisher develops his or her own techniques, and we prefer to do edges with an almost dry brush, and to brush longitudinally with the edge instead of dragging the brush over the edge or molding. Work away from tight corners with your final strokes, but primary strokes can work into corners with a loaded brush. You can tell when a brush is empty, by weight and feel, when it starts to drag differently. At least you can tell with a good-quality brush, but a plastic-bristled cheapie may allow the varnish to run through without control.

When you work a large area, you must maintain a wet edge for the overlap. In hot direct sunlight it can be the test of a good finisher, but you must have the wet edge for the lapping stroke, or else you'll leave brush marks. On a vertical surface this can be difficult and can also require working very fast. Sometimes you can use a foam rubber roller to quickly spread the varnish on the surface, then follow with an almost dry brush for the finishing strokes. This might be a good place

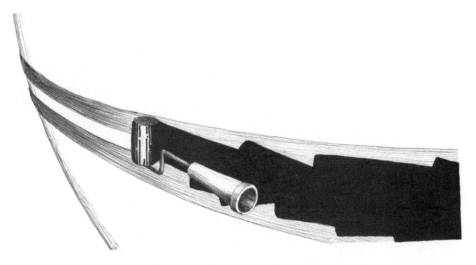

Cut roller covers in half for smaller jobs such as boottops that are in between masking tape.

to use a wider brush to cover as much ground as possible. You can make a rolling pan for the foam roller by lining a tray with new aluminum foil, which will allow you to saturate the roller and roll off the excess over the incline of the tray. Place a block under one end of the tray to keep the varnish in the other end if you're not using a regular paint roller tray.

Foam rollers are completely unknown to many finishers, yet they are a great labor-saving device. The rollers are cardboard with a very thin layer of open-cell foam. The foam does a good job of holding and applying varnish or paint. Foam rollers are clean, and unlike a fabric roller, they leave no stray hairs on the surface, and you can discard them after use, saving cleanup time and costs. We started buying foam rollers to apply epoxy and soon graduated to using them for any number of jobs. The ones we most often use come in 9-inch lengths, and cut into various lengths down to 1½ inches, they work perfectly for varnishing long skinny pieces, such as rails or boottops. They are particularly useful when followed by a brush, which will spread the varnish or paint even more smoothly and also will remove the tiny air bubbles they often leave behind.

Chapter Three

Sanding and Scraping

Sandpaper Types and Grits

If you spend much time finishing boats you'll get to know sandpaper very well, and you may be surprised to learn that there are an astounding variety of abrasive products. Thumb through a manufacturer's catalog, and you'll see the wide range of grades, grits, and types — paper-backed and cloth-backed discs, pads, sheets, wheels, and other abrasive devices. Unless you have special requirements, however, the chances are you'll get by very well with a few basic papers in the 60- to 220-grit range, plus some very fine paper for occasional wet-sanding between coats of varnish. Such a range will usually suffice even for wooden-boat builders; for metalwork and polishing you'd need another spectrum of abrasives.

Every professional builder and finisher has special requirements for types and grades of sandpaper, depending on the types of wood he uses and the boats he builds and finishes. We usually buy sleeves of good fresh aluminum oxide paper, and we try to get sandpaper that hasn't languished on a waterfront storeshelf for years. If you take a little extra care with your sandpaper, it will cut remarkably better. If you buy it from a heated store or warehouse, pop it into a plastic bag until you can get it home. The classic location for keeping sandpaper in a shop is behind the wood stove, and we're no

different. We installed a sandpaper and sanding belt shelf high against the beams and right behind the stovepipe, and it keeps our paper hard and crisp indefinitely.

On board a boat, about the best you can do is to keep your sandpaper in a Ziploc bag with some desiccant thrown in to absorb moisture. Age does not seem to affect sandpaper when it's kept this way, but once exposed to high humidity it will never fully recover its original effectiveness. Cheaper types of sandpaper are especially affected by humidity because the moisture seems to weaken the glue that holds the abrasive to the paper.

We're still using a few small packets of silica gel desiccant that came with a camera we bought years ago. When they get heavy from moisture we bake them in a warm oven for a half hour or so, then throw them back in the sandpaper bag. Cloth-backed sheets and belts seem less susceptible to moisture but are still affected. Abrasives used for wet sanding are probably the most resistant.

We use great quantities of 60-grit paper because we do a lot of epoxy sheathing over plywood; and cured epoxy, especially when silica or graphite is added, is a hard material to sand. We also keep 80-, 100-, and 120-grit; these four handle almost everything. The 120-grit gets used the least, mostly only for interior cabinetry and hardwood that needs a bright finish. Once in a while we like

Abrasive Types

Zirconia Alumina blue

Has a unique self-sharpening
characteristic.

Used for heavy grinding and planing
operations.

Aluminum Oxide brown

Very tough abrasive used for high-speed
work, light duty, and finishing.

Silicon Carbide blue-black

In use, fractures into needle-sharp
particles.

For fast stock removal. Also for grinding
and polishing glass, rubber, and
nonferrous metals.

Garnet red

Made from industrial-grade gems. Slightly
softer than synthetics. Used mostly in
furniture and woodworking operations.

Emery black

Rounded-shape particles. Best for
polishing operations.

Crocus

Soft and short-lived compared with other
abrasives.

Used mostly for polishing metals.

to wet-sand with Watco oil, and we usually
keep a few sheets of 350-grit wet or dry
paper for this.

For varnishing new wood, or wood that
has never been varnished, painted, or sealed
in any way, we start with 80-grit, or even
60-grit if planer marks are evident, and work
through the numbers to 100- or 120-grit. Use
your hand and fingertips as much as your
eye when preparing new wood, since you'll
be able to feel planer marks and imperfections in the surface more easily than you can
see them. There is no better way to check for
unfairness once the sensitivity is developed,
and it takes very little practice. Place the flat
of your hand lightly on the surface and rub
in a circular or longitudinal direction,

anywhere unfairness is suspected. Once
you've developed the technique, your fingertips will often detect what the eye cannot see.
Watch an old-time shipwright fairing the
hull of a shapely sailboat and see how he
uses his hands. Low-angle light also helps,
and moving a light bulb across the surface or
having someone else do it while you watch
will highlight the "wows." If you spot highs
or lows in the surface, you need to sand to
fair first of all; only when the hull is fair do
you sand to smooth the surface.

Sandpaper cross-reference.

Gradations on production (dry) sanding paper
and wet sanding paper are not equivalent.
Equivalencies are as follows:

Production/Trimite Grit	Wet/Dry Equivalent
60	100
80	180
120	240
280	500

Fairing

The finisher must decide the best approach
to each fairing situation according to the
shape, size of job, type of finish, and the
species of wood used in construction. On
wooden hulls, preliminary fairing is often
best accomplished with a plane. A sharp
plane will quickly show any unfair spots,
and although use of a plane for fairing may
come under the heading of building more
than finishing, it can be a helpful technique
not only on traditional plank-on-frame hulls
but also on epoxy and veneer cold-molded
hulls. Once the plane has revealed the unfair
spots, a sanding float or block may be used
to finish the fairing.

Floats or Fairing Boards

For serious fairing, which means radical
wood removal as opposed to cosmetic or
light surface sanding, you will usually need
something more than a small sanding block.
Such fairing boards are sometimes known as
floats (probably because they are designed to

Abrasive Classification

Grit	Use	Grade	Description
20 to 40	Fast finish removal	$3^{1}/_{2}$ to $1^{1}/_{2}$	Coarse or very coarse
60 to 80	Rough sanding and shaping	$^{1}/_{2}$ to 1/0	Medium
100 to 120	Preparatory sandings— softwoods	2/0 to 4/0	Fine
120 to150	Preparatory sandings— hardwoods	3/0 to 4/0	Fine
180 to 220	Finish sanding—softwoods	5/0 to 6/0	Very fine
220 to 280	Finish sanding—hardwoods Dry-sanding sealers and finishes Wet-sanding sealers and finishes	6/0 to 8/0	Very fine, extra fine
280 to 400	Polishing finish coat— all woods	8/0 to 10/0	Extra fine to super fine

"float" over the surface, reducing high spots), or clamp boards, or idiot planes, or one of a host of other names. They do good work in an almost foolproof manner, and a full day spent with one of them will guarantee a good night's sleep.

It takes a bit of experimentation to get the proper shape and thickness of board for each hull shape or surface. We have used floats as thin as ⅛ inch and as thick as ½ inch — the latter hardly bends at all even when long and narrow — but ¼ inch is probably a more common thickness for surfaces of moderate shape. They can be modified in many ways to produce just the right degree of stiffness. Screwed-on handles make them easier to hold, a major consideration during a long day, and handles also may be so devised as to make them selectively stiffer if necessary. A handle can make the float very stiff in one area while leaving it flexible along the rest of its length.

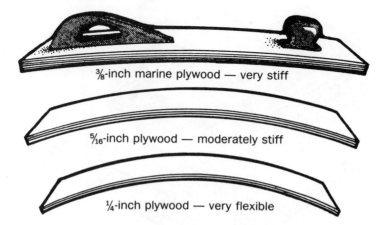

⅜-inch marine plywood — very stiff

⁵⁄₁₆-inch plywood — moderately stiff

¼-inch plywood — very flexible

Flexible plywood sanding floats: vary width, length, and thickness to get the best combination of stiffness and flex for each hull shape. Thicker, stiffer pads provide more fairing action when fitted with sharp, coarse paper. Thinner, softer pads follow the existing contour for surface smoothing action.

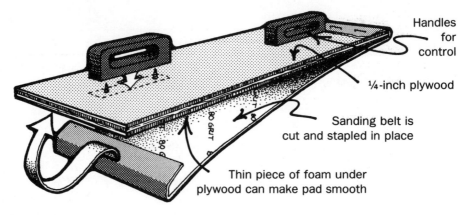

Handles for control

¼-inch plywood

Sanding belt is cut and stapled in place

Thin piece of foam under plywood can make pad smooth

Flexible sanding pad.

A concave or convex handle may also be cut and attached to the float to force it to hold a shape just right for a certain rounded area of a hull or deck.

It is often necessary or expedient to work over the surface in various directions, not just with the grain of the wood. We often use three-directional sanding at such times to remove "wows" in the surface before final sanding and finishing with the grain. We sand flat or level for the first direction, then about 30 degrees to the right, then 30 degrees to the left. Pick an area about 18 inches in diameter and sand through that space with the float held at each of the three positions. Then stand back and look, and finally run your hand over the area.

Such fairing is usually sufficient to remove small highs and lows from the surface; working in three directions both accentuates imperfections and ensures that high spots are removed. Repeat the motion until the area is fair, then move to another area, working methodically over the entire hull. The same type of motion is useful when sanding fiberglass hulls that need fairing

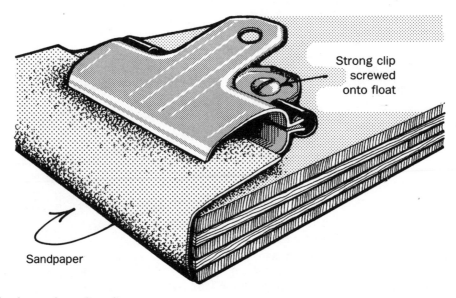

Strong clip screwed onto float

Sandpaper

⅜-inch plywood sanding float.

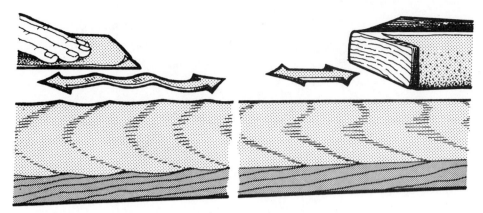

A sanding block helps to prevent the hollowing of softer grain created by hand sanding.

after repair or modification, but the grits used are usually much finer than might be used for fairing wood.

Sanding Blocks

For smaller fairing jobs a block takes the place of the float. Whenever you're dealing with plank edges for example, or the area where stem or transom meets the planking, or sanding over plugged fastenings, a block will ensure a smooth surface. You can make a suitable sanding block out of any piece of scrap wood that's easy to hold. A very short block may only accentuate unevenness on the surface, so the block should be long enough to span a number of imperfections.

To begin fairing with sandpaper, we normally use fresh 60-grit paper wrapped or even stapled around the block or float. Occasionally, to take wood down in a hurry, we use a sanding belt stapled over a block. If you use grit as coarse as 50 or 36, you can expect to do a lot of sanding and maybe even filling to obtain a smooth surface. Keep in mind that it's even more important after such a coarse initial grit to graduate through the numbers to remove the deep scratches. Move to progressively higher-numbered or finer grits, and don't skip any grades in the process or you'll wind up spending much more time trying to remove sanding marks. Smoothness is most critical preparatory to varnishing. Standards can be relaxed somewhat when a surface is to be painted.

If you do a lot of sanding with belts it might be worthwhile to make yourself a block that fits snugly inside a sanding belt with a small wedge on one end. By tapping the wedge in tightly, you can lock the belt in place.

Smoothing

Most amateur finishers, or at least those who are concerned enough to strive for a first-

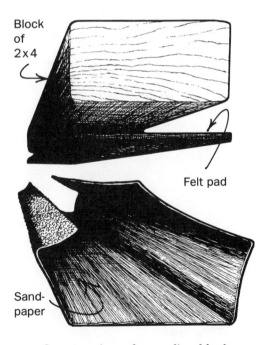

Cross section of a sanding block.

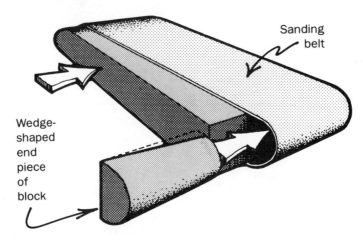

A block with rounded ends can be made to hold sanding belts. One end is cut and tapered to a wedge shape. When tapped tight, the wedge holds the belt in place.

class job, spend too much time and effort sanding bare wood in preparation for applying the first coatings. You need to obtain a smooth surface, but even if you sand the entire hull to a mirror polish with 400-grit paper, after that first undercoating, it'll be much rougher than when you started. Save most of that sanding effort for between coatings. The first coating in particular will raise the grain in places, and will soak in more in areas of loose grain and less in areas of tight grain. Since the purpose of undercoatings is to partially fill the surface, it stands to reason that some sanding will be necessary.

If ribs and planking have been steamed or have been left exposed to sun and moisture, the grain will likely rise considerably more than if the wood had been kept in shade. Whatever efforts you can make to shade your work from the elements will probably pay off, particularly if you live in tropical climates. Hot sunlight is probably more harmful to most finishes and bare wood than is moisture.

For shaped or rounded work a flexible sanding pad will help to avoid flat spots. Scraps of closed-cell foam sheets work well. Without a flexible sanding pad, your fingers are the next best bet. For final sanding of rounded sections such as a caprail, we fold half sheets of sandpaper into thirds and sand

without a block, using our fingers to conform to the shape. By folding the half sheet into thirds (grit should not face grit when folding), you have three fresh, sharp faces to work with; when one dulls, refold the paper to another.

For final sanding before a first coat of varnish, 120 to 180 is usually sufficient. Much depends on the porosity of the wood and how smooth a surface that wood will produce; use finer grits on hardwoods and coarser grits on softwoods that just won't finish finely anyway. There are times when 100-grit is good enough for softwoods, and times when 220-grit isn't really enough for hardwood. Walnut and rosewood, for example, benefit from sanding with a finer grit.

Sand carefully with the grain and take no cross strokes during final finish sanding. Some woods require more care in handling than others. Softwoods in particular — red and yellow cedars, spruce and fir, larch and pine — scratch and bruise easily, and the scratches don't always show until varnish or oil has been applied. Every stroke across the grain or even diagonal to it may show through the coats of varnish.

Wooden masts and spars, because they are often finished bright and are very visible, can suffer from rough treatment in the

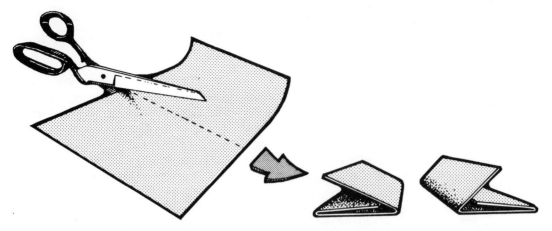

For hand sanding, cut an 8½-inch by 11-inch sheet of sandpaper in half, then fold halves into thirds.

building or finishing process. The frustrating thing about delicate spar woods such as cedar, spruce, and sometimes even clear, dry fir is that often the damage doesn't show until the varnish is applied. Good, dry, spar-grade spruce can be bruised by just dropping it a bit too hard on a bench, particularly when it's a heavy piece. Sometimes even the sticker marks (from the spacers used to separate planks for drying) can be seen in the finished spar after much sanding. There is little or no structural damage, and the only problem occurs when the wood is finished bright. For more on finishing masts and spars, see Chapter 9.

When sandpaper fills with sanding dust, resins, paint, or varnish during use, you can sometimes slap it clean again. Often the abrasive particles are not dulled, but merely gummed up. Even with dry hardwood, it's helpful to give the paper a slap now and again to clean it out. This highly sophisticated technique seems to work equally well with fine, medium, or heavy grits.

Machine Sanding

For large areas, or where old work or new wood must be taken down efficiently and expeditiously, machine sanders are an indispensable labor-saving device. The four types of sanders are orbital, reciprocating, belt and disc.

Orbital Sanders

The orbital, sometimes called a pad sander, makes tiny circles on the work surface. It's good for all finish sanding and works well when sanding uneven grain, such as a miter or scarph joint. Most orbital sanders have a pad that extends slightly beyond the edge of the motor, which allows

Vibrating or orbital sander.

sanding almost flush to a corner, but it will never sand perfectly into a corner. That usually requires some hand sanding or possibly a block.

Most orbital sanders are designed to use either one-half or one-quarter of a standard sheet of sandpaper. We use tin snips to cut a dozen sheets at a time into 48 sections that fit our sander. Cutting the sheets rather than folding and tearing them provides a cleaner edge. Little clamps on the edges of the pads hold a sheet in place, and changing a sheet takes only a few seconds. Make sure you stretch the paper as tightly as possible across the pad so that wrinkles do not appear on the sandpaper as you work.

Reciprocating Sanders

The reciprocating sander goes back and forth rather than in tiny circles and is somewhat less likely to leave sanding marks the way an orbital sander does, but it also works much more slowly. Reciprocating sanders with a firm or stiff pad can sometimes be used to fair a surface. Some sanders will work in either an orbital or a reciprocating motion with a simple flip of a switch.

Flexible pads for these sanders will increase their effectiveness on curved surfaces.

If you can't get one, you can make one from closed-cell foam.

Belt Sanders

Belt sanders are usually big, heavy machines used for fast removal of wood. The continuous belt moves in one direction and must be kept moving constantly to avoid gouging. To remove a maximum of wood, sand across the grain; for finish sanding, the belt should move parallel with the grain. Belt sanders are available in a variety of styles, sizes, power ratings and weights, with belt widths from two inches up. Some are equipped with scavenging systems that pick up some but by no means all of the dust.

It's easy to make a serious gouge with a belt sander, particularly a cheaper model. Novices tend to work too hard when they machine sand, scrubbing the wood vigorously with the sander and bearing down so hard it bogs the motor. Let the sander do the work while you move the machine slowly but constantly over the surface with a steady pressure. When you turn on the machine on a cold morning, let it warm up to full speed (the sound of the motor changes when it has warmed up) before you apply it to the wood, especially if you've just put on a fresh, sharp

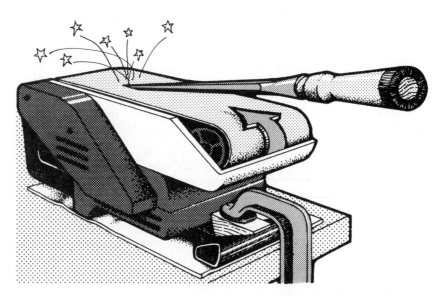

A belt sander clamped to a bench makes a handy sanding tool for small pieces and sharpening tools. Caution: sparks may cause a fire hazard.

sheet of sandpaper. A cold motor and fresh sandpaper may cause gouges in the wood. Similarly, a long extension cord cuts down on the machine's power, causing it to rotate or orbit more slowly than it should for a good job.

At times, sandpaper of any type and grit clogs up after a few strokes. The finish may be too green and need more time to cure completely, or it may need to be wiped down with solvent of some type to remove a surface accumulation of dirt, moisture, or the waxy film that develops when some epoxies cure. High humidity may cause problems. The solution usually is to cure longer, using ventilation and maybe heat lamps; to wipe down the work surface; or sometimes just to get the hull outside in the sunlight, which works best of all.

Buy the best-quality belts you can find; good cloth-bound belts are expensive but worth the money. You'll get many times the amount of work from a cloth-bound belt than from a cheaper, paper belt, and the cloth belt will be less affected by moisture. If you use a belt sander a lot, you can buy specially formulated sticks of rubberized material that, when held against the belt, will clean it. These sticks are available from woodworking suppliers.

Disc Sanders and Foam Pads

These types can do a lot of work in a short time, and can also do a lot of damage in inexperienced hands. When most people think of disc sanders they think of big machines with stiff backing pads and 36-grit discs throwing a shower of sparks across a metalworking shop. Those machines have some application in the boatyard for rough sanding, but lightweight, low-speed machines that will do quality work on a very smooth finish are more compatible with a finisher's needs. For anything but rough sanding, you'll probably need a foam pad, which is the key to the usefulness of a circular sander, at least around boats.

The foam pad is very helpful in smoothing a surface sheathed with fiberglass cloth and epoxy, a primed wood surface, an undercoat, and even smoother surfaces. A

flexible soft pad with fine-grit sandpaper in the hands of an experienced user will caress a surface almost as carefully as hand sanding. A slow-speed sander is preferable on delicate finishes to aid control and prevent the burning that can be caused by coarse grits on high-speed machines. And softer, more flexible pads will not gouge a finely faired surface as easily as hard pads and other types of sanders.

Foam pads often require some experimentation and fine tuning before they work optimally, depending on the shape and hardness of the surface and the concavity or convexity of its contour. Among the wide variety of pads available, some rubber and plastic backings are very stiff and some are quite thin and flexible, while the foam can be a soft, open cell or a thick, firm, closed cell. Small-diameter pads of 5 inches or less are best for tightly concave shapes such as the inside surfaces of hulls, and pads of 6-inch and greater diameter are more efficient and controllable on large flat surfaces. The foam pad on a circular sander is one of the fastest methods for working large areas; although the machine takes more expertise than an orbital or vibrating sander, it rewards the effort of learning.

Whenever we haven't been able to get the pad we wanted, we've made our own. While building boats for two years in the Philippines we made foam pads from our closed-cell Ensolite camping pad. We used contact cement to attach the foam to a hard-rubber backing plate, and used tubes of disc adhesive to hold the sandpaper onto the face of the pad.

Though some finishers get used to big heavy circular sanders, we much prefer the

Foam pad and tube of adhesive for disc sander.

smaller, lighter machines. They can be held overhead more easily, and they can even sometimes be held aloft with one hand to reach a difficult spot. The speed of the motor under load is a big factor in control. High-speed machines may cause you to make more mistakes, and although they will cover more area, they are harder to control. Slow-speed machines also stay cooler and keep the pad and paper cooler.

Sanding discs can be attached by the stud and washer, or they can be glued on with disc adhesive, a type of contact cement that will release without tearing. When we use disc adhesive, we spread the adhesive on a number of discs at one time in preparation for a job, and apply them as needed without having to stop and glue each disc. Remove the disc when you're through sanding, while it is warm, because it will be much harder to remove after it has cooled. When one pad is dull, tear it off and slap on another. You don't lose more than a minute of time getting back into action with a fresh disc.

The sander can leave swirl marks on some finishes, and in these cases it is usually wise to hand sand or perhaps to try another type of machine. Dark gelcoating, for example, can easily pick up swirl marks, even when carefully hand sanded. Green finishes, those that have not yet cured properly, may need more time, heat, or a solvent washdown before they will sand cleanly and without swirl marks. Epoxy surfaces need a solvent wash to remove the waxy coating, and gelcoating should always have a solvent washdown before sanding. A slow-speed machine may solve the problem by eliminating heat buildup on the pad, and it's usually worthwhile to experiment with various grits. New sandpaper may gouge more easily than slightly worn paper, and it sometimes pays to break in a new disc on an inconspicuous part of the hull. On the other hand, worn-out paper will occasionally clog and cause swirl marks. Even the humidity can affect the sanding operation.

Scrapers: Sharpening and Technique

We use scrapers probably more than, or at least as much as, sandpaper. We have a compartment in one large tool box reserved for various scrapers, and alongside that compartment we hang a couple of clean, sharp files just for sharpening the blades. We have an assortment of scrapers accumulated over the years, but generally use just one or two for most jobs. I scrape with just about anything that will do the job at hand, including old plane irons, wide chisels, and sometimes the blade of a lightweight Japanese hatchet that fits my hand just right. For large flat surfaces, I have a couple of thin, rectangular scrapers that get a lot of use. I've filed their corners ever so slightly so they don't scratch or dig into a concave hull side, and I can still use them on convex and flat sections of the hull. Since we do a lot of epoxy work over plywood, mahogany and cedar veneers, and occasionally over fiberglass cloth, the scraper is sometimes both a fairing and finishing tool. We go over every epoxied hull surface with a scraper before sanding, just to highlight the rough spots and remove any drips or dust freckles. Epoxy sometimes bubbles, leaving a tiny, erupted crater as it kicks, and the scraper finds and flattens them immediately.

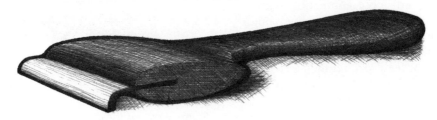

A hook blade paint scraper.

Sharpen scrapers with a file.

For sharpening I put the scrapers in a small vise bolted onto the edge of a workbench and, leaving about ¼ inch of the scraper sticking up above the top of the vise, sharpen straight across, creating a square edge on the blade. This may be slightly different from traditional methods, but it works for us, and instead of one edge I have two sharp edges on each side. I use the scraper all around the perimeter on one side, then flip it over and do the same on the other side. I never bother with a burnisher and never try to remove the burr after filing. We take much more care when working with raw wood that will be varnished, in which case we usually strop the edge of a newly filed scraper to remove the burr. Never sharpen

your steel scraper in or on the boat, because the filings will rust.

We never seem to have much use for shaped or fancy scrapers. I bought some a couple of years ago, but soon gave them to a furniture maker because we never used them. I can't ever seem to find a place that has exactly the same shape or curvature as the shaped blade. I have filed scrapers to shape for use inside the hulls of small boats, but only because we built these same designs over and over and needed a tool for that specific purpose.

One of the toughest scrapers I have is a section of an old power hacksaw blade. It's molybdenum steel and very hard to sharpen, but with a new file it can be done, and the edge holds for a long time even on cured epoxy. A friend gave us three stamped-out rectangles of power hacksaw blade, and with one I made an iron for a tiny wooden plane — once sharp, it stays that way for a long time.

I got tired of looking for my favorite scrapers every time I put them in the tool box, so I drilled a small hole right in the middle of the ones I use most often, and now they stay on the shop wall where I can easily get them.

When you use the scraper, hold it nearly perpendicular to the surface, then lean it slightly toward you, bear down, and pull. If the scraper's small and doesn't provide a sufficient handhold, you can easily make a slotted handle to help. Run a piece of

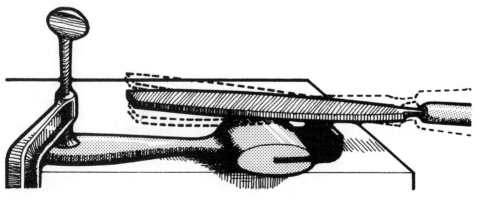

The angle on a scraper blade can be modified for a particular job.

½-inch or ¾-inch plywood edgewise through a table saw. One of my narrow finish table-saw blades is just right to cut a slot that makes a tight push-fit for my thinner scrapers, and thicker carbide blades make a usable slot for the thicker scrapers.

Although we don't often use a curved or shaped scraper, we often need a scraper to fit moldings and caprails with ⅜-inch and ½-inch radius bullnose. Those are the sizes we use most of all, and we found that some old molding plane blades could be modified slightly to make good scrapers for these two profiles. The old plane irons are good steel and hold an edge for a long time. For sharpening these two particular sizes we have Carborundum and India stone slips, small, specially shaped sharpening stones, which do a good job. We use a honing solution of motor oil thinned with kerosene. These blades take a little more time to sharpen, but they hold an edge very well even on tough woods such as iroko and teak.

Scrapers of any type are a fine and often overlooked alternative to sanding. In many cases they are superior to sandpaper and will remove a fine, controlled shaving from the surface without creating dust. Scrapers will also peel a thin shaving from curly hardwoods without lifting grain, and a freshly sharpened scraper will remove stubborn spots of old weathered varnish without sanding.

Dealing With Dust

The tiniest spec of unobtrusive dust, when it settles on wet varnish, will raise a noticeable welt. It will do this until the surface skins over. Dealing with dust is an essential part of any quality varnish or paint job. Still, without the use of one of NASA's clean rooms, you can usually figure out ways to reduce and even eliminate the problems caused by dust, both the kind you see when a sunbeam shines into a darkened room and the heavier, residual dust caused from sanding woodwork.

One way to reduce the amount of dust is not to produce it in the first place. Scrape as much as possible instead of sanding, and don't use electric power tools, which stir up even more dust. A disc or belt sander can fill a room from rafters to floor with dust.

For porous woods that have not been filled, a vacuum will extract dust that no other method will remove. Use the vacuum hose without an attachment to concentrate suction. While you're at it, vacuum the floor to avoid kicking up dust as you work. Even the breeze created by walking through a dusty room will stir up the fine particles into the air.

If you're working on deck, hose down everything but don't splash water on the new wood that's about to be varnished. Turn off all fans and stop all drafts except the ones necessary for ventilation. Just before you begin, use a tack cloth, and keep a clean tack cloth with you to work ahead of the brush. Tack cloths are available from any paint store. Most are cheesecloth or another absorbent cloth treated with a solution that enables them to retain dust on contact. The cloth is folded and presents a fresh face when you refold after a side becomes laden with dust.

You can make your own tack cloths and later discard or wash them. Old cotton handkerchiefs or T-shirts work best. Wash them well, then soak them in warm water. Wring out, sprinkle lightly with turpentine, and pour on two spoonfuls of varnish, making sure these substances are compatible with the paint or varnish you intend to use for finishing. Fold and twist the cloth to mix the ingredients, and keep it in an airtight can to prevent evaporation.

The final step for removing dust specks is your bare hand. Wash your hands and dry them well, and rub down the wood just before you varnish. While varnishing, you can cover the wood one more time with your hand, working just ahead of the brush.

Chapter Four

Brightwork

Brightwork Options

The term, brightwork, means something a little different to each finisher. Some say that nothing else but gloss varnish can legitimately be considered brightwork. Others contend that all naturally finished wood, whether varnished, oiled, sealed, or sheathed, is brightwork. Any transparent finish could be considered bright.

From this wider definition, which we ourselves prefer, a variety of options emerge. Aside from leaving wood unprotected to fend for itself in a marine environment, the other choices for a natural or clear finish are varnish, oil, a combination of varnish and oil, clear two-part urethanes, one-part urethane, various epoxy seals and combinations of epoxy, urethanes, and varnish, or sheathing with lightweight fiberglass cloth and epoxy resin.

To a conscientious boat owner, few things are more satisfying than fine varnished wood. Brightwork is often the standard by which boats are initially judged. When the clear coating is properly applied, it becomes the highlight of the yacht's appearance. Caprails and rubrails, hatch tops, drip rails, dovetailed vent boxes, cabinetry, and a multitude of other items on fiberglass, metal, and wooden boats lend themselves to a bright finish.

The more bright unpainted wood you have on board, the more time you'll spend maintaining it. Brightwork takes more care than painted wood to keep it structurally healthy and to maintain that pleasing appearance.

Natural Weathered Wood

One approach, the easiest at first glance, is simply to leave the wood bare and let it weather naturally. Teak ages quite gracefully under ideal conditions, more so than other woods, and if kept clean will acquire a rich silvered patina. If teak is exposed to wear, oily hands, air pollution, or the occasional dirty deck shoe, however, chances are that instead of that classic silvery glow you'll end up with a scruffy brown color more like weathered scaffolding from a construction site. Conditions have to be near-ideal and strictly controlled to achieve the right look on weathered wood. If your marina is near an airport, for instance, with frequent jet traffic, the pollution will prevent exposed wood from acquiring that antique look. Moderate smog may do the same.

Teak weathers well because of the abundant natural oils, which make it more stable than other woods in a marine environment. Teak is not as structurally strong as some other hardwoods, but it lasts well, resists rot, and has a distinctive look, which make it a first choice for boats and boat trim.

Other hardwoods probably won't weather as gracefully as teak, unprotected or otherwise, and softwoods left exposed are usually a disaster in a short time. Mahogany, oak, ash, walnut, and softwoods such as pine and fir all require more protection from the elements than does teak. Most of them turn black or a disgusting flat brown color from long-term exposure to moisture and sunlight. Aside from appearance, the other problem with unprotected exterior wood is structural stability and protection from rot. While teak will endure far longer than most woods, even teak will suffer eventual degradation from the elements. Those finely fitted scarph joints, bedded, fastened, and sanded so carefully, with matched plugs of aligned grain, will start to drift. Gaps, splits, and cracks will appear, admitting even more moisture, and the process will hasten along. One day you notice the change and realize why so much time and effort is focused on maintenance of brightwork.

Varnish

Until the clear urethanes came along, varnish was the standard of a long-

Brightwork Options

	Ease of Application	Wearability	Longevity	Ease of Removal	Cost	Restrictions/ Remarks
Varnish	Moderate	Moderate	Recoat 2 to 4 months	Good	$8 to $10 a quart	Cures harder than spar varnish
Spar Varnish	Moderate	Moderate	Recoat 2 to 4 months	Good	$8 to $10 a quart	Good sunscreen, stays softer than other varnish
Oil Saturation and Varnish	Moderate, takes more time	Moderate	Recoat 2 to 4 months	Oil can never be removed	Reasonable	Good stabilizing treatment for wood
Clear 2-Part Urethane Paint	Needs proper preparation	Good	Good if properly prepared and applied	Fair	Expensive	Requires a good stable and dry base for longevity
Clear 1-Part Urethane Paint	Same as varnish	Fair to good	Fair	Good	$6 to $8 a pint	Questionable for exterior use
Epoxy Seal with Varnish	Time consuming	Good	Good, but sunscreen must be maintained	Hard	Epoxy is expensive, appx $25/gal	A good basic treatment that will preserve wood
Epoxy Seal w/Clear 2-Part Urethane Paint	Critical and time consuming	Very good	Best, may last 4 years	Hard	Expensive	Both toxic and delicate materials
Shellac	Leaves brush marks	Fair	Good if indoors & kept dry	Good	Reasonable	Very susceptible to moisture
Fiberglass Cloth Sheathed with Epoxy	Difficult	Best	Very good, sunscreen must be maintained	Very difficult	Most expensive	Labor intensive, very strong finish

established tradition of maintaining brightwork, and it remains the most widely used. Varnish can be glossy or mat (satin), and it is more easily applied than the urethanes. Although the finer points of applying varnish require a level of skill, experience, and patience most commonly found at a professional boatyard, almost any conscientious boat owner can produce a satisfactory varnish job.

A good varnish job provides protection from the elements and allows instant visual examination of glue joints, scarphs, and hardware attachments. If these areas were painted, problems might escape the owner's attention until too late for an easy repair.

Spar Varnish

Spar varnish contains various ingredients to filter the destructive radiation in sunlight and lessen the weathering effects of exposure. Mat finish or rubbed-effect satin varnish does not always contain the sunscreen and is more often recommended for interior work, although we have used it with some success for light-duty exterior work if it's properly maintained according to wear and exposure. It never seems to last quite as well as sunscreen varnish, nor will it protect the wood as well.

Spar varnish stays softer and more pliable as it ages, compared with other finishes. This feature is designed into it to allow a better moisture seal in marine environments, as well as a certain amount of flexibility — useful on spars, for example, to prevent the varnish from cracking and splitting. Because of this pliability, spar varnish may not be the best choice for interior cabinetry, or for high-wear areas, such as the rungs of a teak ladder, where a harder finish might last longer.

Spar varnish is as suitable for softwoods as it is for hardwoods. Aside from the treasured look of clean teak with six coats of varnish, it also looks good on Douglas fir and spruce, for example, to which it imparts a warm golden glow that seems to deepen with age. Clear urethanes and epoxies darken the wood with a pleasant patina, as well, but somehow nothing seems to match traditional spar varnish in this respect, especially in the warm light of an oil lamp.

Shellac

Shellac was once a popular choice for clear finishes and as a covering for wood floors. Shellac is made from the secretions of tiny insects that swarm on certain trees in Asia, and the slightly amber color of natural shellac comes from a dye also secreted by the insects. Shellac doesn't lay on as smoothly as properly thinned varnish, and the final brush marks may show, no matter how carefully you apply it. Varnish is sometimes applied over shellac to smooth the brush marks and provide an additional degree of waterproofing. Shellac dries quickly, within half an

Stain Characteristics

	Coloring	Solvent	Application	Drying Time	Bleeding	Grain Raising	Penetration
Wiping Stain	Solid pigment	Water	Brush	6 – 12 hrs	None	Very little	Deep
Water Stain	Aniline dye	Water	Brush or spray	8 – 12 hrs	None	Yes	Very deep
Penetrating Oil Stain	Aniline dye	Mineral spirits or turpentine	Brush and wipe	24 – 30 hrs	Yes	Minimal	Deep
Pigment Oil Stain	Solid pigment	Mineral spirits or turpentine	Brush and wipe	3 – 12 hrs	None	None	Shallow
Alcohol Stain	Aniline dye powder	Alcohol	Spray	$1/4$ – 1 hr	A lot	Little	Deep
Varnish Stain	Aniline dye	Varnish	Brush or wipe	8 – 12 hrs	None	None	None

hour, and within a matter of minutes dust won't stick. Alcohol is used for thinning and cleanup.

Shellac is seldom used now that more efficient and much tougher formulations of varnish and urethanes are available, but is nevertheless still favored by some furniture makers and boatbuilders for traditional authenticity. Shellac can be affected quite easily by moisture (it darkens and will eventually go black), so it is not a good choice for wet areas. Before the advent of epoxy, it was sometimes used as an interior coating for hollow masts and spars, since it was thought to be flexible enough to provide a good moisture seal. Shellac normally has poor resistance to the effects of long-term sunlight.

One-Part Urethane

Although one-part urethane is less expensive and far less temperamental to work with than two-part urethanes, our experience has been that it doesn't work as well for most marine applications. One-part urethanes we have used were designed primarily for indoor use and lack sunscreen.

Two-Part Urethanes

Perhaps the perfect coating for brightwork hasn't come along yet, but the two-part urethanes are one step closer in terms of protection and durability. No clear coating can provide the same degree of protection as paint (because the solids present in paint keep the sun's rays from penetrating to the wood), but clear two-part urethanes can still provide tougher and longer-lasting protection than the best varnish. Clear urethane coating also has fair sealing ability.

Urethanes are, however, at least as susceptible as many other coatings to underlying moisture and wood's natural oils, perhaps more sensitive than some, and for this reason a good seal coat of some type under the clear urethane is necessary for longevity. Most of the clear urethanes were developed for use over pigmented finishes on fiberglass and metal, and unsealed wood does not have the necessary stability. Clear urethane is also more brittle than spar varnish but is more resistant to abrasion.

Although most urethanes were originally designed for professional use and spraying, there are a few that are brushable — an added attraction for most do-it-yourself finishers.

As mentioned before, clear two-part urethane wasn't designed for use over bare wood, so the finisher must provide an effective under seal or base coating for the urethane. The two most common choices for under seals are epoxy and good-quality spar varnish. Epoxy is undoubtedly the better moisture barrier of the two, and since it's a superb glue, it will also add structural support and surface hardness to the wood. Epoxy will not adhere properly to oiled or oil-stained wood, so be sure to get down to clean dry wood before you apply epoxy, removing any existing varnish or seal.

We use at least three coats of epoxy for an undercoat; four or five will build up a tougher coating in high-wear areas. Sand lightly or at least wipe down between coatings. If the weather is warm, you can accomplish three or four coats in one day, applying another as soon as the preceding has kicked. When you seal with epoxy, pay particular attention to end grain, and if possible remove hardware and coat all surfaces.

Three good coats of epoxy on all surfaces will effectively mummify a piece of wood. Small pieces of wood that can be easily unbolted, such as hatchtops and sections of rails, are good candidates for this all-over treatment. Epoxy-sealed wood that is covered by hardware or continually shaded from light and weather will last a remarkably long time without any other coating, but if it's exposed to the sun, it needs ultraviolet protection.

The most common complaint about epoxy seals for brightwork (aside from the extra work) is that the surface may darken slightly more than it will from a varnish seal. It may also turn a deep amber, sometimes uncharacteristic of the natural color of the wood, and some may darken in time, more than varnish, when it's exposed to direct sunlight.

The other commonly used seal for clear two-part urethane is four or five coats of spar varnish, but you should wait two months if possible for it to age before you apply the clear urethane. You can apply the clear urethane over epoxy the next day because it will have hardened already. Spar varnish has a sunscreen, which probably keeps the wood a more natural color over the years, but varnish doesn't seal out moisture as well as epoxy.

Epoxy/Varnish/Urethane Combinations

Yet another approach, which provides the advantages of both epoxy and varnish, is to begin with three coats of epoxy; then apply varnish, waiting at least a day for the varnish to cure (and preferably longer if the weather is cold and damp); then apply clear urethane over the varnish. A little more work, but this finish will see you through possibly four years or more with little more than routine washdowns. If you already have a good solid base of varnish built up that's a few months old, still in good condition, and doesn't need any touching up, then you can sand lightly and apply three or four coats of clear urethane right away.

Teak Brightwork

The very oiliness of teak, and the protective resins that leach to its surface and make it a

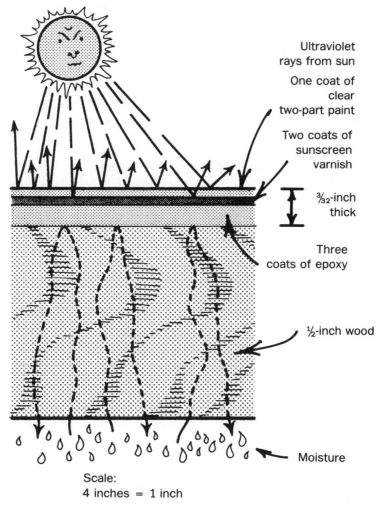

Ultraviolet rays from sun

One coat of clear two-part paint

Two coats of sunscreen varnish

$\frac{3}{32}$-inch thick

Three coats of epoxy

½-inch wood

Moisture

Scale:
4 inches = 1 inch

An effective sun- and moisture-resistant brightwork finish.

long-lasting and attractive boat wood, also make it a little more difficult to finish bright. These resins do a lot to prevent the effective bonds that are easily achieved with less resinous woods. Some finishers feel that teak cannot be properly varnished because of their less-than-ideal experiences with the wood, but with reasonable care, most finishers reach a comfortable compromise and are able to carry off an acceptable bright finish. A glossy lustrous finish on teak is a zenith of the finisher's art. We've used any number of treatments, from leaving it absolutely natural to sealing it with epoxy and varnish covered with a clear two-part polyurethane. We've had difficult jobs but no unusual problems.

Varnish is a built-up surface coating (unlike an oil, which penetrates deeper into the wood) so if you want that deep gloss, you'll need to build up a number of those surface coatings. The trick when finishing teak is to accomplish a reasonable bond between the first seal coats and the top coats.

First, clean the teak thoroughly. Scrub the pores of the wood, with and across the grain, to remove sanding dust and any old finish. Mild teak cleaner and a firm-bristle brush work well. Even teak that looks clean should be brushed with cleaner and rinsed well before varnishing.

The next requirement is a seal coating, which is even more important on teak than on other woods. The seal furnishes a solid base for the varnish, closes off the pores on the surface, and provides a barrier against the natural oils in the wood, which might otherwise discourage a good bond between the varnish and wood. The sealer can be a ready-made preparation, as long as it's compatible with your varnish — or thinned varnish, which penetrates more deeply into the wood. Some finishers cut their varnish with solvent by as much as 50 percent to get the penetration they feel they need with teak.

And some finishers stop right there. The thinned varnish gives a rubbed effect to the teak, instead of a high gloss, and does not make a deck quite as slippery as does a high gloss. Even the thinned varnish will bring up the luster of the natural wood. This is a good, simple, and almost foolproof treatment if you like the so-called satin finish. It holds up reasonably well and after a cleaning can be redone without a lot of trouble. (It's important to clean teak any time you apply another finish, even another coating of the same finish, or else you'll end up with a gummy mess in the pores of the wood.) The nice thing about this system is that you can go ahead and apply your final coats of varnish if you decide you want more gloss after all.

For those who do want to go a step further and apply glossy varnish, build up a number of coats and follow with regular maintenance. Even if you've built up a substantial number of coats, plan on sanding lightly and applying a couple more coats every two or three months to keep it up, especially on flat areas exposed to the full force of the sun — and make sure to choose a varnish with a sunscreen for these applications. No sunscreen presently available will entirely mitigate the effects of long-term direct sunlight, but it will undoubtedly extend the life of the finish and preserve the health of the wood as well. Varnish will make a teak deck slicker than will an oil finish. Even a traditionally caulked teak deck will be slicker with a few coats of gloss varnish, though some go ahead and choose appearance over usefulness or safety. In any case, when you work on a flat surface, resist the temptation to flood the surface with heavy coats rather than building up multiple lighter ones.

Clear two-part urethane is very effective over teak — and even more promising in terms of longevity. As is always the case with two-part urethane application, preparation is vital; with teak this is doubly true because of the oils and natural porosity of the wood.

Two-part urethanes are particularly susceptible to cracks in the finish, such as along caulking lines in the deck or against scarph joints. Anywhere a crack appears moisture will enter, work its way underneath the finish, and lift pieces of the urethane right off the teak. More information about urethane finishes can be found in Chapter 7.

Another of the more stable finishes for

teak is an oil-saturation treatment, which is allowed to dry thoroughly and is then varnished over. We apply thinned linseed or Watco teak oil in at least three separate applications, wiping the excess away after each application. Waiting at least a day between applications and waiting at least another day after the last treatment before varnishing will usually show possible problems with spots of bleed-back. If we have the time, we wait as long as a week for the first varnish coating, which is thinned slightly; subsequent coatings are full-strength. The oil helps to stabilize the teak and also promotes a more effective bond to the surface coatings. The oil also darkens the surface somewhat.

Our favorite method for handrails and other teak trim is a good cleaning, followed by three coats of epoxy, then unthinned varnish or clear two-part urethane for a sunscreen. The epoxy gives the teak a deeper amber hue. This treatment, however, makes a very slick surface and is sometimes not the best choice for decking, but it wears well.

Working with Varnish

Varnish and Weather Conditions

The weather, which you can do very little about except to watch and enjoy, becomes a variable to be reckoned with when finishing, particularly in less-than-ideal climates or seasons. Modern-day formulations of varnish seem to be a little less susceptible to bad weather conditions than did the varnish we used 20 years ago, when we never varnished

Characteristics of Various Treatments for Wooden Masts

Product Type	Ease of Application	Abrasion Resistance	Durability	Toxicity	Cost
Oil	Easiest of all: just sand and brush on oil coatings	Minimal	Even the best oilings need to be redone every year; may also attack scarphs and glue lines.	Low	Least expensive
Enamel Paint	Moderate	Fair	Fair	Low to average	Moderate
2-Part Polyurethane Paint	Requires more preparation and care than other paints	Good	Very Good	High toxicity	Two to three times higher than enamel, plus additional preparation
Varnish	Moderate	Low	Fair: depends on preparation, number of coats and climate	Low	Comparatively inexpensive
Epoxy Seal and Varnish	Epoxy seal takes moderate preparation before varnish	Epoxy resin alone has good abrasion resistance; varnish must be properly maintained.	Excellent if varnish is maintained	Epoxy catalyst has high toxicity	Expensive
Epoxy, Fiberglass Cloth and Varnish	Most labor-intensive	Best available	Best, but varnish must be maintained	Epoxy has high toxicity, but very safe after cure	Most expensive and time-consuming

For better results on a chilly day, heat the varnish in a pan of warm water before using. Make sure that the can is at least partially open.

on cloudy days and never too early or too late in the day. But it's always a good idea to let the morning dew evaporate before you start, and wind up a job well before sundown, long enough to allow the fresh varnish to skin over before the evening moisture settles. The approach of a weather front with an increase in humidity is reason enough to procrastinate another day, but dry cloudy days have never noticeably affected the gloss of our varnish jobs. Varnishing in high humidity might seal in more moisture than usual, but since varnish is a semipermeable coating the extra moisture won't cause disastrous problems, although the varnish may take longer to cure. A *sudden* increase in humidity (or drop in temperature) might cloud the varnish, and if these changes are associated with the approach of a frontal system, there could be problems with rain spattering the varnish. But wind is usually the worst problem. It blows drop cloths around, swirls dust, and ruins your concentration.

You can deal with cold weather by allowing the sun to warm the wood as much as possible, using windbreaks if necessary to improve the solar effect, and we have often resorted to warming the varnish beforehand. Try placing the *slightly opened* can in a pan

of warm or hot water for an hour or so before you start brushing. *Don't heat a sealed can.* Space or electric heaters may help bring the wood up to temperature, particularly if you can rig some kind of enclosure. A small, inexpensive hygrometer will give you a much better idea of relative humidity and will also make you aware that colder air can carry a

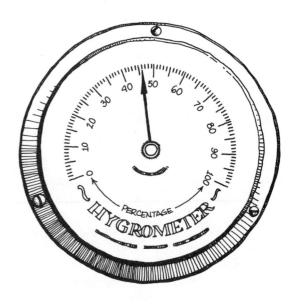

A hygrometer measures the humidity (moisture) in the air.

deceptively large amount of moisture. The hygrometer is particularly useful when you are using moisture-sensitive materials, such as epoxies and two-part paints. Weatherband radios are handy for up-to-date forecasting and can be a useful part of a finisher's tool kit.

Recoat Times

A difficult and time-consuming part of a good varnish job is to remove all sandpaper grit, sanding dust, and lint. Failure to do this will ruin a perfect varnish job and will become more apparent in successive coatings. By recoating at the right time you can sometimes avoid this sanding and cleanup.

We once applied six consecutive coatings of spar varnish to the sheathed topsides of a cold-molded 30-foot hull, from boottop to rubrail, without touching a scrap of sandpaper from the first coat until the last. There was ample preparation beforehand, of course, and the epoxy-sealed surface was a perfect stable base for the varnish. The entire six coats went on in a day and a half. The finish survived almost a year of hard service, and although there were the usual dings and scrapes on the hull, we got through without a touchup. The hull was varnished in a closed, heated shop, which solved the problem of changing weather. We did the entire job with foam rubber rollers, cutting in, touching up, and smoothing behind the roller with a good-quality 2-inch brush. The 9-inch-wide roller helped to quickly cover the large area and provided good control, especially when we used an inclined rolling pan to load the roller. The saving in labor over brush application, sanding, with cleanup between each coating, was substantial and demonstrates the potential of taking advantage of recoat times, without having to sand between coats.

Optimum recoat times vary somewhat according to temperature, humidity, air circulation and sunlight, so any recommendations we might offer are approximate guidelines for making your own decisions based on working conditions. You must wait a long enough interval for the varnish to

Read the can labeling for manufacturer's recommended recoat time.

bond properly to undercoats and to skin over so that your brush or roller doesn't drag on a still-wet coat, but if you wait too long the next coat will not bond properly to the undercoat. This may sound more complicated than it really is, and common sense along with a thorough reading of can labeling will usually see your project through without problems. Exposure to bad weather can make recoating a guessing game, and conditions have to be good to accomplish it without a closed, heated shop.

Mixing Techniques

A friend who owns a yacht maintenance business turns all his paint and varnish cans end-for-end every other week. It keeps solids from settling out and prevents having to stir so much just before use. Paint can be shaken in the can before the can is opened — in fact the more the better — but clear finishes should not be vigorously agitated because this causes bubbles. New varnish and first coats may require thinning, so some stirring is inevitable but should be gentle and slow to prevent aeration. Stir from the bottom of the can to the top, and use a clean flat-bottomed stir stick.

Use the original can for storage only, and never thin in the storage can, or dip into the storage can with a brush. You can punch holes in the rim of a can to prevent drips down the side, but this will prevent using the can for long-term storage because it will admit air.

Careful finishers never pour varnish back into the storage can, but if you must save the varnish, you can strain it through a filter or nylon hose, the longtime favorite filter of finishers.

Try not to pour more than you'll need from the storage can, and never fill the mixing pot more than half full, so you'll have more control for wetting and wiping the brush.

Dip only the tips of the bristle in the thinned varnish, and very gently spread the bristles against the side of the mix pot to unload the brush slightly. Do it gently to prevent creating bubbles as the varnish runs back down the side of the mix pot. The bubbles stay and are lifted out again by the next brushful. Hold the loaded brush upside down while you move it from the can to the work, to keep it from dripping.

Many varnishers use the two-can method, keeping on hand a collection of small cat food or tuna fish cans (thoroughly washed, of course). One can is used for the fresh varnish and the second can for wiping the brush between every dip to get rid of dust picked up from the surface. The first can is never reused but is replaced with a new clean can. If you want to be thrifty, you can save the recycled varnish in the second can for rough jobs, but most finicky finishers will just throw it away.

On final coats, which are the most critical if you want a flawless job, try to use a newly opened can of varnish, pouring about an inch in the bottom of a clean can. When a can of varnish gets about two-thirds used, the remainder isn't for finish coats and should be used instead for temporary touch-ups or preliminary coats, which are less critical.

Varnish Seals

Even when working with fresh new wood, many people don't bother to apply a specific seal coat under the varnish. A seal will increase the life of a good varnish job, sometimes by a factor of two or three. Without some type of seal under your varnish, you're leaving it more vulnerable to a host of moisture and ultraviolet-related problems, such as peeling, lifting, chipping, hairline cracks, discoloration, and even sometimes the beginning stages of dry rot.

Purists sometimes choose not to seal

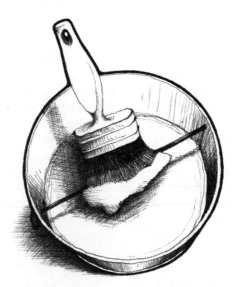

"Tapping off" the brush on the paint can rim sometimes causes bubbles in the finish. One way to avoid this is to insert a length of coat hanger through the top of the can.

under varnish for various reasons, one of which is that there can be noticeable differences in the finish. An oil seal will darken the wood somewhat, but is the easiest type to apply. For traditional work an oil seal is a good choice since the oil penetrates deeply into the wood and provides improved long-term stability, increasing the effective life of the varnish overcoating. As with oil applications of any type, an oil seal needs to be wiped "tight," or very dry, using folded sections of an absorbent cloth and wiping repeatedly until the surface is as dry as possible. This surface should be left for at least a day before varnishing and sometimes more if the weather is less than warm and sunny.

An epoxy resin seal may change the hue of the wood somewhat — it gives teak an amber glow over a period of time — but is the best in terms of providing a good waterproof base coating. Epoxy must be applied over a clean, dry wood, and varnish can be applied the next day, after the epoxy has cured and has been scrubbed with soap and water and lightly sanded.

A wood-pore seal is actually just a filler that provides a smoother surface. It doesn't really seal the surface of the wood from moisture and also requires some skill to apply and sand down. It can change the appearance of the surface, particularly if it doesn't perfectly match the wood.

Varnish manufacturers recommend mixing one part of appropriate thinner, or thereabouts, with four parts of varnish for a first coat. This is a good idea even on sealed wood because it helps the varnish to flow better and provides a transition coating with better grip. A 1:4 dilution is the minimum advisable for unsealed wood; in fact, on unsealed wood it might be worthwhile to repeat this process a second time before using full-strength varnish for the top coats.

Repairing Varnish Damage

Scrapes and scratches are inevitable and should be repaired as soon as possible to prevent harm to the wood. A fresh scratch is easier to repair than an old wound, for once the weather gets to it, the damage will be harder to cover without stripping to bare wood.

Temporary damage control consists of touching up with fresh varnish as soon as possible, and for this reason many boat owners keep a small can of varnish at hand. You can quickly seal a scratch when it happens and come back later to fine-tune the job. A boat owner we know covers fresh scratches immediately with a piece of tape, which seals out water and also makes the scratch obvious until repaired.

When time comes for proper repair, it's simply a matter of sanding the area and feathering out the edges for successive coatings of varnish. For final coating after the scratch or scrape is filled, sand a successively larger area and apply fresh varnish for the final coating.

Some varnish work may be so far gone

Tape can temporarily protect varnish damage and acts as a reminder that repair is necessary.

that the most logical approach is to strip it and start from the beginning, as with new wood. The original varnish may not have been properly applied in the first place, never filled, sealed, given enough coats to be effective, or just not maintained. You may find white spots where varnish has separated from undercoats, or black areas where moisture has gotten to the wood, or deep scratches from normal wear and tear. With luck the darkened areas are only surface blemishes and will come around with vigorous scraping and sanding, but if they don't, if the damage is deeper, you probably have three options — to stain, bleach and stain, or paint. Short of painting the wood, you can try to disguise the blackened area with a heavy application of filler, at least to the extent that it matches the rest of the wood without sticking out like a sore thumb. But this is probably only a stopgap measure for a problem that will return and become worse. You should attempt to solve the problem that caused the blackening in the first place. For example, one of the most difficult areas to seal from moisture, over the long term, is a butted section of handrail or caprail where a vertical or angled section meets a flat or horizontal section. Moisture runs down the inclined section and collects on the butt joint, eventually finding its way through the varnish coatings and into the end grain of the rail, where over a period of time it proceeds to turn black. The solution, other than laminating an entire section of rail and eliminating the butt joint, is a more efficient glue or caulk, perhaps an epoxy to provide a better and stronger joint. All this then requires covering with multiple coatings of varnish, but once the work is done, you've achieved a *solution,* not just a stopgap.

Removing Old Varnish

Removing old varnish down to fresh wood can be a straightforward or a very difficult task, depending on the age, location, and condition of the varnish, the shape of the surface, and the health of the wood beneath. Aged, sunbaked, and thin patchy areas of old varnish are perhaps the most difficult to remove, particularly if they are clinging to a curved surface. Such weathered areas are also usually mottled from uneven exposure to sunlight and moisture; they will require vigorous scraping and sanding to bring up a fresh and consistent surface. Less weathered areas of varnish and areas of varnish that are still providing a good seal will be easier to remove by gentle scraping and sanding. It's important to keep the scraper sharp at all times for better control and removing caked varnish more easily. A dull scraper requires more pressure, increasing the chance of its damaging the wood, or slipping off and scratching other parts of the boat.

Coarse sandpaper is acceptable only if you're willing to work through the numbers to remove all the scratches. Sandpaper is not always the best initial method for removing varnish unless the varnish is so decayed and flaked that it comes right off. In that case, a scraper is still quicker and will do less damage. Sharpen a scraper as fine as you can, and you'll be able to take a fine shaving right down to the wood. If you're using a putty knife, round the edges slightly so you won't gouge the wood surface. Finish with sandpaper only after you've scraped all the old varnish away. A fine-grade metal file will remove isolated spots of hard varnish and prevent you from sanding deeply into the wood while you try to remove one obstinate spot. A very sharp block plane set fine may work, or maybe a Surform tool for an especially stubborn spot, although you can do a lot of damage with such tools. Belt sanders seldom make sense for varnish removal. They're hard to control and it's easy to gouge the wood underneath. Use a belt sander only for large flat surfaces, where you can afford to sand off a lot of material.

Paint remover will soften the old varnish and make it easier to scrape off. Brush it on heavily and give it time to work. You may need to repeat the application if all of the varnish doesn't come off the first time.

Heat also works well to loosen old varnish; even a hot noonday sun will make varnish a little easier to remove. Heat guns and heat lamps work sometimes and make scrap-

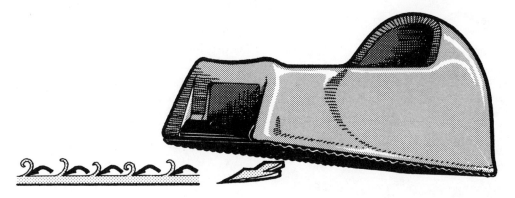

Surform blades have hundreds of teeth with openings that let shavings pass through.

ing easier. A propane torch used with great care may help stubborn spots, but an open flame is very dangerous, especially around paint, varnish and solvents.

Additional Surface Preparation

Bleaching

Bleaching is a technique most often used on old work that has been stripped for new varnish. Sometimes part of a rail has been under shade or a cover, or maybe wear has caused a change in the natural uniform colors. Don't rely on a finish coat of varnish, oil, or any transparent finish to provide a uniform shade to wood that is obviously mottled. If anything, a clear finish will accentuate the discoloration. Bleaching is sometimes required even on new wood if it's been exposed unevenly to sun or moisture and has developed a weathered or inconsistent look. Even wood stacked on stickers for drying will often show marks where stickers were laid.

It's good to understand what you're doing when you bleach wood, because bleach is a strong chemical that can damage wood. Natural oils come to the surface of wood to protect it from the elements. They oxidize to a sometimes classic silvery color, especially on teak. Bleaches remove these oils and soften and weaken the wood surface. They eat away softer grain, attacking softwoods more than oily hardwoods. Certain woods with abundant surface oils will not bleach evenly since the oils and resins resist the bleach. Pine is a good example, and Douglas fir can cause problems in selected pieces and cuts where the resinous rings are exposed. Tropical hardwoods, such as yacal, iroko, and apitong may require extra care.

One point often overlooked is the necessity to neutralize the surface of the wood after using strippers or bleach, which is a good suggestion for any kind of refinishing. Acids left in the wood after bleaching can streak the wood surface — and may not show up until after the new finish is applied, gradually becoming worse as the acid works on the wood and new finish. A solution of soda ash or borax will neutralize bleach and halt further action, but must be generously applied to every part of the bleached surface to be effective. It should be applied with a brush or a saturated rag and then rinsed well with fresh water; repeat the procedure as many times as necessary to ensure that the bleach is neutralized. (Two separate washdowns with the neutralizing solution, followed each time by a vigorous rinse is good insurance.) If the wood is especially porous or open-grained, you may wish to scrub the neutralizing solution into the wood with a stiff bristle brush, working with the direction of the grain.

Almost everyone bleaches teak; in fact, some finishers feel that bleaching is necessary to achieve a better bond for the varnish, probably because of teak's oiliness.

Rinse deck thoroughly after bleaching.

Softer wood, such as pine and fir, are bleached much less than colorful dark and oilier woods, such as teak and mahogany. We once bleached some strips of iroko, a wood similar in some ways to teak, in order to match it to other pieces on a rubrail, and the results were satisfying. Bleaching, like staining, is usually an attempt to obtain uniformity, and some areas may need stronger, longer, or repeated applications in order to match.

After stripping and cleaning the wood in preparation for bleaching, use drop cloths and any other method you can devise to protect decks, fiberglass gelcoatings, aluminum, and other wood. Bleaching solution will etch aluminum and dull gelcoating. Flush everything with water as soon as possible when bleach spills. You may want to keep a water hose handy in case of accidents. Some people wet down the decks ahead of time, which dilutes the bleach in case of a spill and gives more time to flush it with fresh water.

Work in sunlight, and try to keep all surfaces to be bleached in sunlight during the entire bleaching process. Turn the boat if necessary. Consistency is what achieves the best results. A cold, damp, shaded section of handrail will react differently from a sun-warmed section. Give the darker, worn, or most mottled parts of the wood the first applications of bleach, then work your way over the rest of the wood. If possible complete each section, and don't stop in the middle of a piece.

Follow specific instructions for the bleach you're using. We've seen fair results from Clorox, mixed with 85 percent water by volume, as a starting point. You can make your own solution by buying oxalic acid crystals (available in marine and paint stores) and adding the crystals to warm water. Stir until they stop dissolving, and you'll have a good strong solution. Dilute if it's too strong. If you use oxalic acid, let the solution dry on the wood, then brush with a stiff bristle to remove the remaining surface powder. Brush this powder onto a drop cloth and away from anything it might damage. Then wipe or brush on a neutralizing solution of soda ash or borax, as described earlier, to halt further bleaching. Let the wood dry, and for the first time you'll get an idea of how effective your bleaching operation has been. If it's the right shade and if you're sure it's neutralized and rinsed well, then resume sanding and preparation for the first varnish coat. Keep this first sanding dust washed off the boat because it will still spot vulnerable areas. If some areas need more bleaching, carefully repeat the process. Let the wood dry completely before you make your final decision. Look at it in strong light.

Bleaching is not the healthiest thing for wood and should be used only as necessary. Bleaching properly is not a demanding or extremely critical operation and reasonable care will see it through. Work with small jobs until you get a feel for the process. As with all chemical reactions, bleaching is affected by various factors. The duration of the reaction or treatment is an important consideration; the longer the treatment is applied, the more effect it will have on the surface. Temperature affects bleaching in that the warmer the temperature, the stronger and more effective the bleaching action. This is very evident when working in a hot midday sun. The temperature of the wood surface and of the bleach itself also affects the speed of the chemical action. The strength of the solution is another prime factor in speed and effectiveness of bleaching. When working with unfamiliar bleaching agents and solutions, it's always wise to experiment on a small sample patch, perhaps in a less visible spot, to establish the appropriate time and strength-of-solution parameters for your situation. If in doubt, dilute until you are confident with the mixture.

After bleaching, rinsing, and drying, some raised grain will be left, which needs sanding. It's important to use fresh, dry sandpaper for this.

If you're bleaching heavily stained old work, try to remove as much of the stain as possible before bleaching. Before working with potentially dangerous formulations, try soap and elbow grease. Scrub vigorously with a strong soap (or an abrasive soap with pumice, such as Bon Ami), using a tough pot scrubber pad. These pads are almost like sandpaper; they will scrape the surface, but they may be just the thing to renew old wood surfaces. A solution we once resorted to was a paste of Fuller's Earth (or French chalk) as an absorbent, and carbon tetrachloride as a solvent. Carbon tet is a very dangerous chemical that has now been removed from the market, but plain paint thinners might be almost as effective. Paint or wipe the solution on the stained area, gently wire brush, and let it dry. If the treatment is effective, it may be repeated a number of times. Oil stains are generally more resistant to removal than water-based stains, but old stains of any type can be very stubborn. In the worst cases, the only solution may be to replace the wood itself.

In lieu of mixing your own solutions, you can buy one of the two-part products available in marine stores. One part contains a cleaner and the other a bleaching solution. The cleaning solution by itself is worth the money, for often a good cleaning is all that's needed, particularly on wood exposed to frequent handling or pollution. Always clean the wood well and then have a good look when it's dry before you decide whether or not to bleach. Oftentimes bleaching isn't necessary, much to the health and longevity of your wood.

Staining

If a section of wood is discolored from exposure to sunlight and moisture, if your sanding has uncovered a lighter area in older

Ingredients for the bleaching operation.

wood, or if you want a more uniform hue to the wood before varnishing, stain may solve these problems. You'll need to stain the entire surface, but you can exercise a fair amount of control over the match by wiping on more stain in lighter areas and letting it set longer before wiping. If that doesn't work, then repeat the application on lightest areas, and blend as well as possible into the rest of the surface.

When using a stain for the first time, practice on a scrap section, or at least start on a less visible area until you get a feel for the process. Even the same brand of stain may vary from can to can or have more or less thinners, which will lighten or darken the mix. Stain, once applied, can be difficult to remove because it penetrates. You can always add more to darken, so move forward with caution, wiping immediately until you're familiar with the stuff. If there are oily spots on the wood, try wiping with trisodium phosphate and rinsing to remove the spot before you stain. Oil-based stains require at least a day of drying time.

Apply stain with brush or rag. A brush is usually easier to control, but some experienced finishers prefer a rag because they are able to cover a large area more quickly, with less likelihood of dripping the stain. A brush is best for small moldings. Brush or wipe the stain with the direction of the grain, and when you get a uniform coating, let it stand

for a few minutes until it appears to flatten, then wipe. We'll say it again; practice beforehand!

Arm yourself with several good, heavy wiping pads or cloths, the kind that will take the scrubbing and not leave lint on the wood. We learned from experience not to use old cotton diapers because though soft and very absorbent, they leave lint and fuzzballs everywhere. Old cotton towels are good; less absorbent dishtowels provide even more control; and old flannel shirts that are not completely threadbare work well. Some finishers prefer burlap for its strength and absorbency.

If you wish to accentuate the grain in the wood, wipe mostly with the grain, but if you're striving for a uniform surface, try wiping across the grain and diagonally.

If you've waited too long to start wiping and the wood appears too dark, try wetting your wiping pad with thinner and scrubbing. Scrub vigorously in darker areas and you may be able to lighten them if you haven't waited too long. Once you've achieved the desired shade, or as close as you can, let it dry; then have another look later. When it's well dried, sand the wood lightly with a fine-grit paper to remove any raised grain, taking care to sand with even strokes all over the wood. Vacuum or otherwise remove the sanding dust, and you're ready for the first coat of varnish.

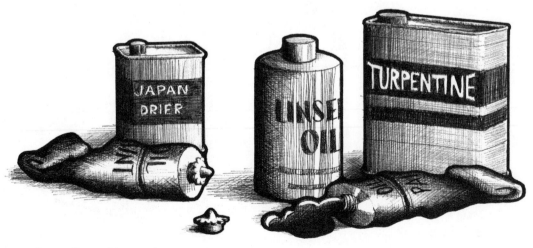

Ingredients for making stain.

You can mix your own stain, using three parts boiled linseed oil, one part turpentine, and one-half part japan drier, an additive that accelerates drying time. Buy a tube of burnt umber oil paint for the base color, and raw umber or brown for blending in small amounts to match your wood. Test rub your mix on a scrap of your own wood until it's right. Keep in mind that linseed will slightly darken the wood, so if you want just a slight darkening, perhaps linseed alone will be enough.

Some wood fillers contain stain, and stain can be mixed with the filler to accomplish filling and staining in one step — though gaining proficiency at this operation requires a bit of practice. By using the appropriate thinners (water, mineral oil, or paint thinner) on paste filler you can achieve the required consistency and color. More thinner added to the stain will reduce the filling qualities, but you'll need a thicker paste for porous wood. Be careful with dark stains because they blacken wood and small amounts sometimes go farther than you might expect.

Fillers

Any wood with large, open grain or hollow pores will need to be filled or smoothed if you wish to achieve a glassy finished surface. Mahogany, for example, has tiny holes that will create depressions in the finished surface, whether varnished or painted — and this is even more true of the cheap lauan grades now often sold as mahogany. Almost all woods can benefit from a skillful job of filling, if only for the sealing effects, though certain woods, such as oak and ash, seem to require less filling because they are very hard and light-colored.

Paste wood fillers are available that will very closely match the color and texture of most commonly used species. Fillers should be used on clean new wood, although we have gotten away with using them on previously oiled wood if its surface was unusually porous. Try to match the color of the filler as closely as possible to the color of the wood. Softwoods, such as fir, prefer a neutral or natural filler; most hardwoods usually require dark fillers.

Sometimes you have to make your own filler. When filling grain flaws in a Brazilian rosewood cabinet we had a problem matching filler to wood until we collected rosewood sanding dust from a belt sander and mixed it with thinned filler for a near-perfect match.

Mix the filler paste, a small amount at a time, with the recommended thinner (usually turpentine) and brush the mixture onto the wood. Brush in all directions, paying more attention to porous areas. Try to stipple the filler into the wood in areas where more is obviously needed. Most fillers need to be wiped when they turn dull — and don't wait too long! It's always best to try the filler on a

Most Effective Wood/Stain Matches: Hardwoods

Wood	Best Base	Best Color
Ash	Any	Any
Basswood	Water	Reddish brown
Beech	Water	Reddish brown, maple
Butternut	Water	Walnut, oak
Cherry	Water	Red to brown
Chestnut	Oil	Red to brown
Ebony	Water	Reddish brown
Elm	Water	Red to brown
Gum	Any	Maple, walnut
Mahogany	Water	Red to brown
Oak	Water	Greenish brown
Rosewood	Water	Reddish
Teak	Oil-Water	Brown
Walnut	Water	Walnut, maple

Most Effective Wood/Stain Matches: Softwoods

Wood	Best Base	Best Color
Cedar	(seldom successfully stained)	
Fir	Oil	Brown
Hemlock	Oil–Water	Red to brown
Pine	Oil–Water	Brown
Spruce	Oil–Water	Amber

piece of scrap wood for match and consistency before applying it to prepared wood.

Some finishers prefer to wipe the filler on with a clean rag, but we like the better control of brushing, and the filler is easier to remove. You can always repeat the process, but if too much filler is applied, you have to sand to remove it. The idea is to fill all the pores and holes in the wood, then to remove all the excess from the surface. You'll need to sand, but very lightly, to bring up any surface, and you should use final-grit paper to avoid taking off too much wood. Take care to sand only with the grain of the wood. Sand too much, and you'll sand the filler off and have to start over again. Paste fillers should be used only on porous wood and small, shallow scratch repairs. Paste filler is nonstructural and will crack if used in large globs.

It's a good idea to fill one day and varnish the next, to let the filler dry overnight. It's also a good idea to get away from the job after filling and have a fresh look at it in the morning. You can often spot something you missed the first time around.

Keep the filler covered so it won't dry out. It needs to flow well enough to wet the surface. If it dries during use, add a few drops of thinner until it's right again, and on

Commonly Filled Woods

Wood	Best Mix	Best Color
Ash	Heavy	White to Brown
Beech	Thin	Red to Brown
Butternut	Medium	Light Brown
Cherry	Thin	Brown, Black
Elm	Heavy	Brown
Mahogany	Medium	Red Brown
Maple	Thin	Natural
Oak	Heavy	Brown
Rosewood	Medium	Red to Black
Teak	Heavy	Brown
Walnut	Medium	Brown to Black

a hot day add thinner every few minutes. Get all the dust off the wood before filling — vacuuming draws sanding dust out of the pores of the wood. If the filler mixes with too much dust, it won't stick.

Plugs

The subject of plugs perhaps belongs more appropriately in a book on construction than in one on finishing. We have included it, however, because most finishers eventually have to deal with wood plugs, whether it be to remove and replace pieces of

Plug
cutter
bitt

Leftover wood is ideal for plugs and may be matched to specific areas on the boat.

trim (or structural members), or to fill and seal existent screw holes in the process of surface preparation.

The traditional method for filling screw holes is to plug them. For large jobs you may wish to buy a substantial quantity of pre-made wood plugs, but for smaller jobs we usually make them ourselves with a plug cutter and scrap pieces of wood left over from building the boat. On some fancy boats finished bright, we often mark and save cut-off hood ends of each plank to make matching plugs for the individual planks. One of the little plug cutters that fits into a drill chuck is usually sufficient and does a good job if it's sharp. The drill can be hand-held and the cutter plunged into scraps of wood clamped to a workbench. The best way, however, is to use a drill press, which is safer and will allow you to better utilize all the wood, and with more control.

If your building stock is 1-inch thick and you need ½-inch-deep plugs, there is a simple way to make a lot of plugs in a short time. Rip the one-inch stock into strips two or three inches wide, and cut the plugs into the wood from both sides. After cutting all the plugs on both sides, put the stock on the band saw and rip it exactly in half. The plugs will almost fall out of each side.

Plugs are normally installed with the grain parallel to the planking. This also facilitates trimming the plug, which is done

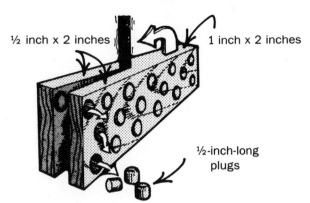

Rip stock in half after cutting plugs for a quick way to double the number of plugs.

with a chisel at least twice the width of the plug's diameter. Lay the chisel bevel-down along the hull, against the plug and $\frac{1}{16}$ inch (or more) above the surface, and give it a light tap with the palm of your hand. As the plug splits off with the grain, you will immediately see which way the grain is running. If necessary, you can move to the opposite side so that you won't chip out the grain under the surface of the hull. This will very quickly become apparent in practice, and is another reason for laying the plug grain parallel to the planking. You then know the grain must be cut in one of two directions.

On small, delicate hulls that are to be

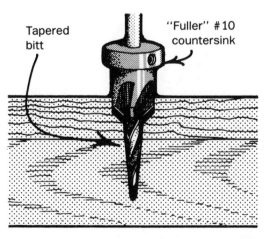

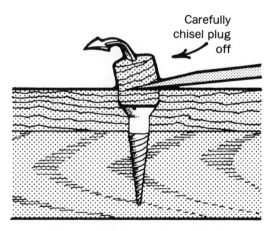

Plan ahead for filling screw holes by drilling with a tapered bitt for the fastening and a countersink for the plug — all in one operation.

finished bright, we cut plugs flush with a sharp paring chisel. The paring chisel doesn't have the heft of a larger, framing chisel, but it will slice thin layers of grain from the plug until it's flush. On very large hulls, plugs are often cut with a sander, but on smaller hulls we try always to cut the plugs flush first, so that only a light sanding with a block is required before the undercoat or varnish is applied.

How you choose to glue in your plugs depends on whether they must ever be removed again. If not, a plug dipped in a small flat pan of epoxy and a drop of epoxy dabbed into the hole will hold forever and keep water from the fastening underneath, as well. An acid brush often works best, and be careful to keep the epoxy off your hands by wearing surgical or rubber dishwashing gloves.

Weldwood glue, resorcinol, or even white glue is a better choice if the plug will require removal later. Plugs glued this way are easily removed later by drilling a small pilot hole in the middle of the plug and then inserting a screw in the hole. As the screw bottoms out on the head of the screw already in the hole, it will lift out the plug — or at least pieces of the plug, which will allow you to clean out the hole. Plugs on sacrificial rubbing strips on the side of hulls may just

be rolled in bedding compound and tapped into place. The bedding compound will provide a seal, and the plug will remove easily for access to screw or bolt heads.

Holes, repairs, defects, and fairings on the hull need to be filled with something that will stick tenaciously without shrinking or swelling; that will seal the area from water absorption; and that can be sanded. Epoxy is the only material that will do all these things well.

For filling screw holes, we prefer a thickened mixture of epoxy and microballoons (more on this in Chapter 5). Larger or deeper holes may need to be filled in two steps. If the application is a critical one, start by slathering the area with unthickened epoxy, which will provide the best bond; then apply a thickened mixture of microballoons with a pinch of silica.

Holes as shallow as ⅛-inch may also be effectively plugged and sealed by gluing in the plug with epoxy, leaving it overnight to cure, and then carefully shaving the plug flush with a paring chisel. If you want a permanent seal to the fastening below, apply a drop of epoxy with an acid brush and then apply the plug. The plug cutter normally cuts a slight taper on one end of a plug, and this is usually inserted into the counterbored hole. Very shallow holes may need to be

Drill a pilot hole in the plug to be removed, then insert screw. As the screw "bottoms out" on the fastening below, the plug is lifted out on the screw threads.

*Very shallow holes may need to be plugged with the un*tapered *end of plug, left to dry, then shaved.*

plugged with the untapered or straight-cut end of the plug.

Holes that are too shallow to accept a plug should normally be glued with epoxy, but there are occasional exceptions. The quarter-inch planking on an ultra-light cold-molded pram of double diagonal construc-tion was too thin for a plug, so we set the few fastenings required just below the surface and filled them with catalyzed clear epoxy resin. (The hull must be upside down to do this.) The silicone bronze Phillips-head screws glowed in the bright-finished red cedar and became a very attractive feature of the boat.

On a hull that's to be painted, screw holes, chips, scratches, or dings may be filled, using a clean, sharp putty knife. The putty knife should be flexible. Too many of the new putty knives seem stiff, but if you look around you can usually find a good knife at a paint store.

After using your putty knife for epoxy work, wipe it clean before the epoxy cures, then come back the next day with a sharp paring chisel and shave the film of epoxy off the blade of the knife.

Chapter Five

Epoxy

Epoxy resins have been around since about 1945, at first used primarily for military and industrial applications. Most people are acquainted with epoxy as tiny squeeze tubes seen in hardware stores and hobby shops, but during the last 12 to 15 years, epoxy has become a popular boatbuilding material with amateurs and professionals. Epoxy is used as a glue between wood veneers in cold-molded hull construction, and is also widely used for repair of polyester resin–fiberglass hulls. And as we have seen already, it makes a highly desirable sealer for wood because unlike polyester resins, varnish, and most paint, epoxy is an effective moisture barrier, Various formulations of epoxy, with differing characteristics, are available; they have varying degrees of moisture tolerance and toxicity.

Epoxy can be applied with a brush, roller, or squeegee. A foam-rubber roller is a particularly efficient way to cover a large area with a uniform coating. Disposable acid brushes and cheap foam brushes also are suitable for small, quick jobs. A squeegee can be used to spread resin quickly over a large area and can be used on vertical and sloping surfaces with care. Squeegees, like plastic mixing cans, are cleaned by simply leaving them to kick and then squeezing them to pop the hardened epoxy loose. This leaves a clean surface that may be used over and over again.

One gallon of epoxy, applied at normal temperature to a smooth surface, should cover approximately 500 square feet of surface area. Foam roller application is best, since it's difficult and tedious to brush a uniform coating of epoxy over a large surface area. A properly applied coating of epoxy will be approximately 3 mils thick, and three to four coatings will be necessary to achieve a thickness of 10 mils, which is recommended for sealing a fiberglass hull bottom under the waterline. When sealing wood above or below the waterline, we try for a minimum of three coatings for long-term effectiveness.

Epoxy/Fiberglass Sheathed Brightwork

Yet another option for brightwork, where maximum toughness, structural support, and resistance to abrasion are desired, is to sheathe the wood with a lightweight fiberglass cloth using epoxy as saturation and bonding resin. Not only will this provide the best protection possible for a clear finish, but lightweight fiberglass cloth, when properly applied, is almost invisible.

Sheathing suits a variety of finish requirements. We have used it on the six steps of a teak ladder leading to the bridge of a charter boat, which allowed them to be finished bright and still wear well. (The weave on a sheathed surface can be left un-

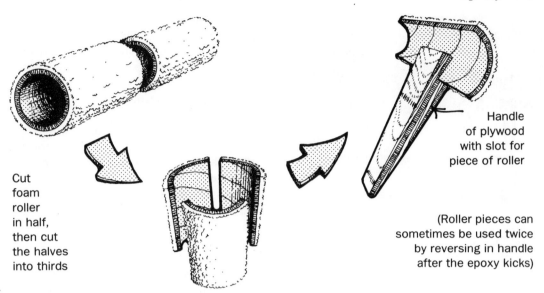

Cut foam roller in half, then cut the halves into thirds

Handle of plywood with slot for piece of roller

(Roller pieces can sometimes be used twice by reversing in handle after the epoxy kicks)

A "Jim Watson brush"; very effective for smoothing a finish — cheaper than foam brushes, with more control.

filled, which will provide a good surface grip.) We sheathed the caprail on a small bulwark around a dive boat to protect it from weight belts and diving tanks. We sheathed the caprail on our own sailboat and covered it with the same clear two-part polyurethane used on the cold-molded wood hull. Other areas that can benefit from this treatment are handrails, natural wood transoms, large wood vent boxes, and other areas where wear is a problem. In addition to brightwork, many hull and deck areas are also candidates for sheathing. Traditional plank-on-frame wood hulls, however, are not the best candidates for sheathing because they absorb lots of moisture and will not provide the dry and stable base necessary for long-lasting sheathing.

Cloth and Resins

Fiberglass cloth is sold by weight (ounce per square yard), which is a guide to its thickness and strength. Four-ounce cloth, for instance, is quite thin, lightweight, and easy to saturate with resin. It makes a fine sheathing for small boats and for areas where weight is a consideration, but it adds only minimal abrasion resistance and

strength compared, for example, to a double-layer sheathing of 10-ounce cloth. The weights we normally use are 4-ounce, 6-ounce, 7½-ounce, and 10-ounce. Sometimes only a small increase in weight, such as from 6-ounce to 7½-ounce, will produce a major difference in the heft of the cloth. The weave on a 7½-ounce cloth is much more visible, and it will take a lot more resin to wet it. Six-ounce is a fine middle of the road choice for bright-finished cold-molded hulls that need some protection and sealing. Properly applied it will be virtually invisible, adding only a slight opacity to the wood.

Fiberglass cloth must be stored in a dry place and kept out of direct sunlight. We store our rolls overhead, on 1-inch dowels or pipes tied to the roof beams. The rolls are easily lowered by untying one end. Fiberglass rolls should not be stacked on end, and it's a good idea to cover them with plastic or paper when they're not in use in order to keep out the dust. If fiberglass is allowed to sit in the sun, absorb moisture, or get dirty or stretched, it will not become uniformly transparent when you saturate it with resin; cloudy areas will appear in the finished surface. If you are in doubt about a roll of

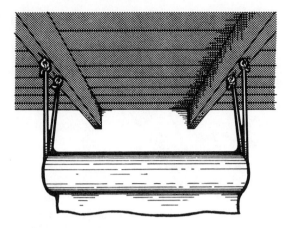

Fiberglass must be stored with care. Never set a roll on end or leave the cloth exposed. Hanging it works well.

cloth, do a test section to make sure that it saturates well.

Although two basic types of resins are used in boatbuilding, epoxy and polyesters, in our experience only epoxy is really suitable for sheathing. Polyester just doesn't have the necessary long-term bonding ability, and many attempts at sheathing with polyester end in peeling. The sheathing starts to loosen, and as more moisture is admitted, it will peel right off a hull in sheets. Polyester is most suitable for laminating fiberglass hulls, where multiple layers are used and the exterior is usually protected by a relatively moisture-proof gelcoating.

Epoxy resin will bond tenaciously to clean, cured polyester resin, but polyester will not achieve the same bond when it's used over cured epoxy resin. Epoxy is more than twice as expensive as polyester resin, but compared to the overall cost of the boat, that amount is usually negligible. We store our epoxy resin out of the sunlight, but cold temperatures don't seem to bother it much; we keep ours all year long in a shop that sometimes gets well below freezing and have seen no ill effects, at least from the brand we use.

Mixing Epoxy Resin and Catalyst

Unlike polyester resins and catalyst, epoxy must be mixed in exact proportion to attain the proper reaction. The cure of polyester resin in colder weather can be accelerated by simply adding a few more drops of catalyst to the mixture, but this is not the case with epoxy. Temperature and high humidity can be critical. We try not to work with epoxy when there is more than 60 percent humidity. Different formulations have different degrees of sensitivity to moisture. If you have to work in a humid environment, we strongly recommend that you purchase a resin that's more tolerant of moisture. Consult manufacturers to find out which type is best for you. We do almost all our epoxy work in a wood-heated shop, but anyone who is forced to work outside in the weather will have to pick his or her work times and resin more carefully.

We always use a metering pump for mixing epoxy resin and catalyst. These pumps are available from epoxy distributors in a number of types and sizes, from mini-pumps that screw right into the can to large, industrial models that dispense pre-metered resin and catalyst in gallon-sized doses.

If you're doing a lot of epoxy work, buy a box of tongue depressors from the local drugstore to provide a plentiful source of clean mixing sticks. When the epoxy is metered into the mixing container, give it a thorough mixing; if you have a tendency to mix too little, count out 50 or 75 strokes when you mix. Scrape the bottom and sides of the mixing container.

Plastic mixing cans in large and small sizes are available from epoxy distributors. After the leftover epoxy kicks, the container can be squeezed, and the hardened epoxy will drop right out.

Working Safely and Comfortably with Epoxy and Fiberglass

Safety considerations are important whenever you work with fiberglass and epoxy. Fiberglass is, after all, *glass:* misery if it settles on your skin, dangerous if it gets into your lungs. The catalyst for epoxy resin is highly toxic; it should be kept strictly off hands and used only with adequate ventilation. Barrier creams, gloves, safety goggles and organic fume respirators are essential

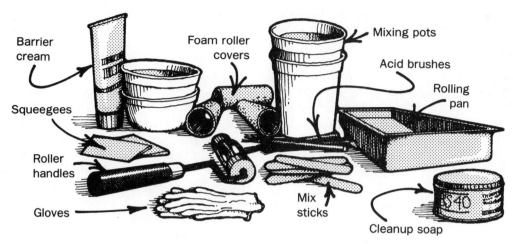

Tools for applying epoxy.

for protection. We make a real effort to "work clean." Unless by accident, we never allow the resin to touch our skin. In addition, and to alleviate some of the concentration of dust and fumes, we use electric fans in the window and doorway to create a draft, moving fumes and dust away from the work area and thereby reducing, by a degree, some of the hazard involved in working in close quarters with such dangerous materials. Careful planning can eliminate almost all the grinding and sanding from the sheathing process, which will make your environment and temperament a lot more pleasant. Use planes and scrapers instead of sanding whenever possible. When feathering a cured edge of fiberglass cloth, use a block plane set fine to take off the bulk of the material. This is best done soon after the epoxy has kicked and is still somewhat pliable and easy to cut. Planing creates no dust at all and provides more control and fairing action than a disc sander. Following the planing, whatever sanding must be done will be minimal.

Cotton clothes are without doubt the most comfortable against the skin for fiberglassing work and should be thrown away after the job is finished, since anything worn for fiberglassing work will retain some of the dust through a number of washings and will probably never again be absolutely free of the dust. Old flannel shirts with rubber bands on the sleeves and high button

necks are good protection next to the skin, and a large cotton bandanna around the neck may help. Over all this inner clothing you can wear complete coveralls, such as the excellent disposable types available for lab and shop use. Polyester resin will usually wash out, but once catalyzed epoxy resin touches your clothes, it will harden into an inflexible spot that will eventually break into a hole.

Surgical gloves will protect your hands during small jobs, and you can discard them after use. Rubber dishwashing gloves will last longer if you wash them clean of resin after each use. Try rubbing a few drops of

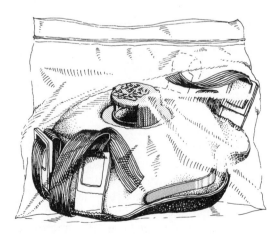

An organic fumes respirator should be kept sealed away from the air.

liquid soap or barrier cream on the gloves before use, and they'll be easier to clean later.

If you're planning to start a big fiberglassing job first thing in the morning, you might forgo a shower the night and morning before. Leave all the natural protective oils on the skin. Barrier cream is good on your hands, arms and neck, anywhere you are liable to get an itch. Use it in particular between your fingers and up your wrists.

Preparing the Surface

Before epoxy/fiberglass sheathing can be applied over wood, the wood must be bare, clean, and dry; oiled or stained wood will prevent the epoxy from bonding at its best. Epoxy/fiberglass sheathing adheres well to clean, dry fiberglass that has been saturated with polyester resin, and it will stick to sanded gelcoat if the gelcoating is healthy and has been properly prepared. Epoxy/fiberglass sheathing can also be applied to aluminum, but the surface must first be prepared by sanding or etching with acid to create a suitable base for a good mechanical bond. Metal preparation kits are usually available from epoxy dealers.

If the underlying surface to be sheathed is very porous, as in the case of red cedar or spruce, it should be sealed with a coat of epoxy resin and allowed to cure, then lightly sanded before the fiberglass cloth is applied. This will prevent areas of resin starvation, which may turn whiter than surrounding areas and also not adhere properly. After sealing, the surface should be sanded or scraped lightly to remove dust particles and small bubbles. Running your hand over the surface is the best way to find these small bumps and craters.

Applying the Cloth

Applying the cloth and saturating it with resin is a relatively simple procedure, easily learned. The operation is most straightforward on large surfaces, either flat or gently curving, such as cabin sides and coamings. On the other hand, the larger the area to be sheathed, the more cloth and resin you will have to manage, so smaller projects are usually best for first-timers. If the piece to be sheathed is removable, such as ladder rungs, you will save yourself a lot of masking and cleanup, and the project will be more accessible on all sides.

Four-ounce to 6-ounce cloth can be shaped fairly easily to most surfaces, but if it has to wrap around a sharp corner or a very tight radius (less than 1 inch), it will have a tendency to lift off the wood surface, leaving a void beneath. One solution to these spots of lifting and bubbles is to let the resin kick, sand or plane the lifted cloth away, then roll or brush on a number of coats of resin to fill the void. Properly done, this will be almost invisible, and the resin will provide additional protection to the spot. Applying cloth to reverse curves can also be very difficult due to the pulling and stretching involved; it may be best to do complex pieces in smaller sections.

The two most commonly used techniques for applying fiberglass cloth are the so-called dry and wet methods. In the dry method the fiberglass pieces are positioned while still dry, then saturated with a coat of epoxy. The wet method involves rolling on a coating of catalyzed epoxy, applying the cloth over the still-wet coating, then applying more resin to the surface to complete saturation. A third method involves presaturating a section of cloth in a tray or on the workbench, then applying it by hand to the wood. This presaturation method can be messy unless your're adept, but it's good for small pieces or cramped spaces inside a boat. It's still a good idea to roll a coat of resin on the wood before applying the saturated cloth.

The dry method is considered easier for first-timers because positioning can be accomplished without the additional pressures of dealing with wet resin and saturated cloth. It does, however, involve a bit more work, for the cloth can only be saturated from the top down. If you're using the dry method, particularly over soft or porous wood, the surface should always be given a preliminary seal coat to prevent resin starvation as you sheathe.

Vertical and overhead sections can be dry-sheathed using staples, tacks, tape, or

Traditional varnished brightwork.
(Chapter 4)

Naturally finished wood.
(Chapter 4)

Varnished and natural teak side by side.
(Chapter 4)

Varnished wood.
(Chapter 4)

Fiberglass/epoxy sheathed bright-work. (Chapter 5)

Varnished mahogany. (Chapter 4)

*Fiberglass/epoxy sheathed brightwork.
(Chapter 5)*

Unsheathed epoxy. If a boat is not intended for hard use, epoxy alone, without the fiberglass sheathing, will yield a handsome finish while keeping weight down. (Chapter 4)

Fiberglass/epoxy sheathed brightwork.
(Chapter 5)

Bright mast with hardware.
(Chapter 9)

An oil soak can prevent splitting of timbers.
(Chapter 6)

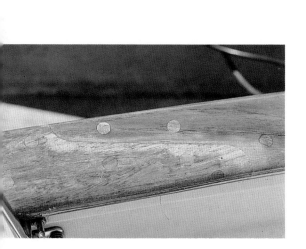

Repairs to caprail and rudder
need stain to match.
(Chapter 4)

Boottop and sheer stripe artistry.
(Chapter 13)

Applying masking tape for stripe layout. **Left:** *It takes a keen eye to judge the fairness of a hull.* **Right:** *Apply the tape in sections, smoothing well.* (Chapter 13)*

Fiberglass bottom blisters under treatment by sanding and epoxy. (Chapter 15)

Unsealed fastenings bleeding under paint. Before painting, fastening holes that are too shallow to accept a plug should normally be glued with epoxy. (Chapter 4)

Poor preparation under paint job. (Chapter 1)

Wood joint separating under paint. Another problem easily solved by using an epoxy sealer. (Chapter 5)

Polyester resin filler shrinking. Epoxy resin is more than twice as expensive, but will prevent this annoying problem. (Chapter 5)

A 2-inch Chinese bristle brush (left) compare with cheap synthetic bristle (right). (Chapter 2

A scraper for every occasion. (Chapter 3)

Surgical gloves, plastic mix pots, and tongue depressors for mixing sticks make an epoxy job neater, safer, and more accurate. (Chapter 5)

Red microballoons (left) and colloidal silica gel (right). (Chapter 5)

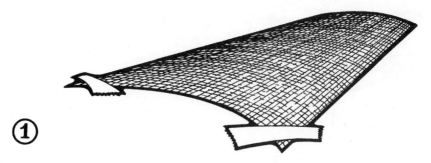

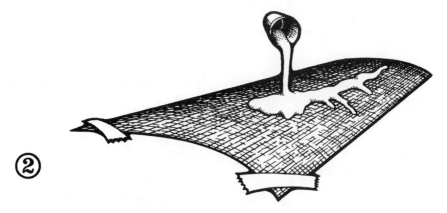

①

For dry sheathing method apply cloth, cut to size, and if necessary, hold in place with staples or tape.

②

Pour or roll well-mixed epoxy resin over cloth.

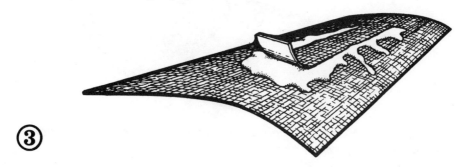

③

Squeegee resin over cloth, using a foam roller to achieve uniform saturation. Remove tape as you work, but staples may be left until the epoxy kicks.

battens to hold the cloth in place while saturating; even so, they may require a nimble effort. After saturating the cloth, you can make very minor adjustments to correct positioning, but if you pull too hard the cloth may drop off. If you need to trim the edges, it's best to wait until the resin starts to kick before you cut because it's easy to pull the wet cloth out of position.

The wet method is our choice for most sheathing operations because it gives slightly better bonding. The challenge lies in situating the cloth just right on the wet wood — an even trickier feat on a curved surface. Once the cloth touches the wet surface, it sticks and can be slid and moved around only with care and some difficulty. If you pull too hard in one area, you will separate the weave

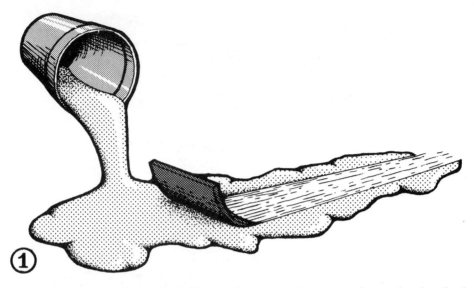

For wet sheathing method, pour mixed epoxy resin onto surface to be sheathed and spread evenly with squeegee or foam roller.

While resin is wet, carefully apply cloth and position it for final saturation, using foam roller, squeegee, or gloved hands.

of the glass cloth. To apply a large piece of cloth over a prewetted surface, it's best to roll it on from a mailing tube or broomstick dowel, rather than trying to unfold it right onto the surface. If you get it right, the first time, the process will go fine. But if the piece goes on sideways, or with wrinkles, you'll have to smooth it first, then roll on sufficient resin to complete the saturation process before the catalyzed resin starts to kick. Give yourself plenty of time by starting early in

the day when it's still cool, or by using slow-hardening catalyst.

The selvage, or bound edge, of fiberglass cloth leaves a noticeable bump on the surface when saturated with epoxy resin. When two edges of cloth meet, you have the option of either lapping one over the other, or making a simple butt joint. A small lap gives better continuity and strength, but leaves a welt or bump in the surface that must later be sanded flush. Even a butt joint does not

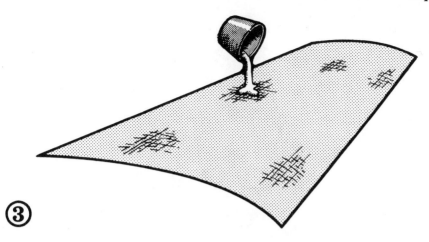

③

Apply more resin where needed to complete saturation, using squeegee and roller.

always fit perfectly and may require filling with more epoxy resin.

Whether you're fairing laps or just cleaning a cured edge, a few careful passes with a sharp block plane will show the high and low spots. After planing, sand if necessary with a long block, starting with fresh and sharp 60-grit paper and working through the grades to 100-grit or 120-grit. Fiberglass and epoxy cure into a very hard surface, and if you get to it a short time after the cure is complete, fairing will be much easier.

Epoxy Fillets

A fillet is a concave or shaped fairing applied in corners, such as where a bulkhead meets a side of the hull, or where the deck meets a sheer clamp. Epoxy fillets are structural, forming a web that will increase hull stiffness. They are also watertight. They have a very pleasing appearance when painted over, and they complement good shapes to make a structure look "organic," as though it had been formed from a single piece.

Epoxy fillets are so abundantly useful when building and finishing a boat that it's hard to imagine how we got along without them. Mostly what we did was to spend a lot of time messing around with fiddly little moldings, caulkings, and sealants, trying to

reinforce and make watertight all those angles where components and cabinetry meet.

It's not that fillets are radically new; we used them years ago with polyester resins. Back then they were usually a mixture of sawdust, sand, asbestos, and various other floor sweepings. The idea was sound; the fly in the ointment was the polyester resin, which swelled, shrank, cracked, and wasn't really a very good bonding resin in the first place. Epoxy changed all that. It's a tenacious glue and does not absorb moisture. With the readily available variety of fillers, you can now engineer a fillet to match almost any requirement.

Epoxy fillets may be used on fiberglass, wood, and aluminum hulls. Wood surfaces must be dry, unpainted, and unoiled: in other words, bare, clean wood. Fiberglass gelcoating should be removed if there's any doubt about its condition. Aluminum must be well sanded, grease-free, and dry. For critical applications on aluminum, an acid etch is recommended.

The fillet is applied with a paddle made to the appropriate radius; a gloved finger may work best for small sizes and tight places. The fillet conforms to almost any fixed or changing angle, and may be applied overhead as well as on vertical or horizontal surfaces. We normally apply the fillet mix-

Fillet paddle designed for two commonly used radii. Sand smooth all edges of the ⅛-inch plywood paddle before each use.

ture straight from the mixing bowl with a putty knife or fillet paddle. For long small fillets, try cutting the top third from a balloon, filling it with the mix, and using it like a cake decorator to squeeze the mix into the groove, to be followed immediately with the fillet paddle. You may also just dab the mix in place and follow with the paddle, working short sections at a time and pulling, not pushing, the fillet paddle along in contact with both sides of the joint. If you've mixed the ingredients in the right proportion and consistency, the fillet will be smooth. Once applied to satisfaction it should be left alone. Add extra material *later,* if needed in low spots, by sliding the paddle over the surface again,. You can also vary the thickness and profile of the fillet by tilting the paddle slightly, a necessary technique if the angles are not constant where the paddle meets both sides. When the fillet is the way you

want it, clean the excess from the edges by scraping with a sharp putty knife. Then leave it alone to kick.

Although a number of fillers are available for specific functions, we use red microballoons and colloidal silica almost exclusively for epoxy fillets. Both are available from any number of mail-order and boat-building supply houses and also from many epoxy suppliers.

Silica is used for a high-strength mixture where weight is of little consequence because it's very dense and heavy. Silica fillets are also nearly impossible to sand — almost like trying to sand a pane of glass.

Red microballoons form a lighter filleting mixture that is still strong enough for most applications. It's best as a cosmetic and can be sanded and painted. Even when making low-density microballoon fillets, it's a good idea to use a small amount of silica to

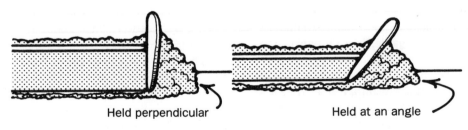

Held perpendicular   Held at an angle

The width and depth of a fillet can be varied by turning the paddle while working the mix.

Clean excess epoxy off immediately after finishing the fillet. A sharp putty knife works best.

promote a smooth-spreading slick consistency that helps in applying the fillet.

We vary the ratio of silica to microballoons according to the application. For our white-water river dories, which take a lot of abuse and are held together exclusively by epoxy fillets reinforced with fiberglass cloth and tape, we use the following mix: ten pumps of epoxy from a standard pump mixer, three scoops of microballoons, and seven scoops of silica. Our scoop is equal to two rounded tablespoons. It always seems to take some experimentation to arrive at the best ratio for each job, and the temperature of the resin also will affect the filler-to-resin ratio.

Larger fillets will sometimes have to be formed in two or even three stages. They require a lot of material, and once the epoxy starts to catalyze, it gathers momentum rapidly. For this reason, small batches are more manageable, and in hot weather they're necessary to provide the time to apply, spread, and clean up the epoxy properly.

For critical applications, such as on our river dories where the fillets hold everything together, we sometimes start with a silica-enriched mixture and then reduce the percentage of silica in subsequent layers, ending up with a microballoon-rich mixture that sands easily.

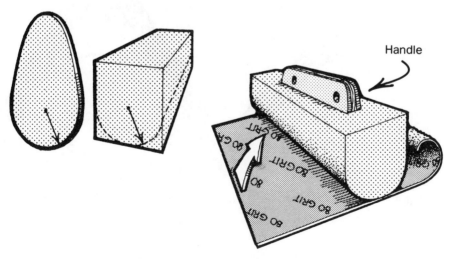

To make a fillet sanding form, use a block plane to shape a piece of wood to the same radius as the filleting paddle (left), then wrap with sandpaper (right).

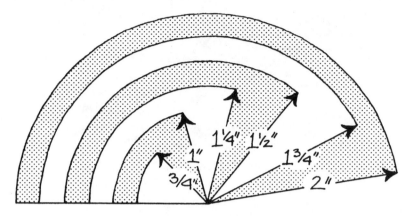

Examples of actual size radii.

For sanding fillets you can sometimes find or make a dowel of the proper size. For larger sizes you can often attach a handle to the sanding form by gluing on a short piece of plywood. Wrap a piece, or half a piece, of sandpaper around the form and hold the edges under your fingers where it can easily be rotated slightly as sections of the sandpaper dull. Finish by hand sanding on edges and corners; the fillet is then ready for undercoat and paint or fiberglass tape.

We sometimes use a radius as large as four inches and possibly slightly larger for certain applications. Depending on the angle at which the two pieces meet, you can put in a large or small amount of filler. Large fillets look great but must be properly applied and finished. They provide a surprising amount of structural support to a joint, and waterproof it too.

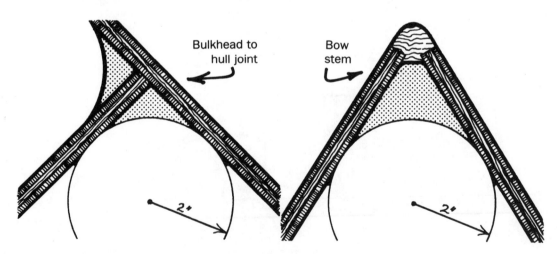

Differing amounts of fillet material used for different angles but with the same radius.

Chapter Six

Oils

Oiling is the oldest method for preserving wood. Oil waterproofs and stabilizes, preserves natural unpainted wood, and forms a good underseal for paint or varnish when they're compatible. Oils penetrate the wood grain more deeply than any other treatment — as much as ¼ inch on flat grain flooded repeatedly with thinned oil, and up to ½ inch or more on end grain, even with tight-grained hardwoods such as teak. (End grain sucks up oil about as fast as it's applied and should be given as much as it will take for maximum stabilization.) That kind of penetration does a lot to protect the wood and make it repell moisture.

Oils don't always keep the surface of wood looking new; in fact, none that we know of will maintain that fresh look very long without regular maintenance. Oils, however, go a long way in protecting the basic health and stability of wood. Water, combined with sunlight, is what causes breakdown of the surface cells in wood, and a heavy application of oil is one of the best choices for limiting this weathering action. Resins, waxes, and stains in various oil formulations also help protect the surface to varying degrees and produce a variety of finishes.

Types and Formulations

Dozens of formulations and combinations of oils are available. Oils are thinned to im-prove penetration, various compounds are added, and you'll even find "secret" formulations containing resins, driers, and stains for better performance.

A nice thing about oil is that it combines the warm, sensuous feel of the wood with a surface coating. Tight-grained hardwood, properly sanded and oiled, will have the luster and feel of silk. Oil can be satin, hand rubbed, or glossy according to the resins added and the way it reflects light. The more gloss, the less natural the wood feels.

For an oil to be successful it must, except in special circumstances, be a drying oil, and not remain sticky like common motor oil. Driers can be added to oils such as linseed and tung to accelerate or improve their drying characteristics. These drying oils form a solid barrier in the wood that cannot be dissolved away, unlike varnish or paint.

Linseed is the most widely used oil, and tung is probably the next most popular. Linseed is refined from flax seed and is found in a multitude of popular brand finishes, mixed with various amounts of thinners, driers, stains, and resins. Linseed must be refined ("boiled") to dry properly because raw linseed will stay wet for months. Linseed is popular among traditional woodworkers, and some actually enjoy its distinctive smell. They also accept the fact that linseed darkens and yellows the wood somewhat. Some boatbuilders use raw linseed as a saturation coating, and in some instances this may provide more protection than processed or boiled linseed because it stays sticky longer. But it also gets very dirty.

Tung oil comes from the fruit of the tung tree. Marco Polo has been credited with bringing tung oil to Europe from China, where it was used as an all-around sealer. The great wall of China was supposed to have been sealed with tung oil, which may account for some of its longevity, but that sounds like advertising copy. Some finishers stick loyally to either linseed or tung, each extolling the merits of one over the other. Tung oil is slightly more water-resistant than linseed. Pure tung oil may be heated to produce a polymerized form, which dries faster and provides slightly better luster than the pure form, and which is preferred by some finishers.

Linseed and tung oils are also used to create a separate category of oils called Danish oils, a name derived from oiled Danish furniture. The oil is mixed with various synthetic alkyd and natural resins and stains to produce distinctive finishes. The resin additives range from tree sap and insect derivatives to the newest urethanes.

For years, boiled linseed mixed 50/50 with kerosene has been used by builders of wooden boats as a *soak* solution. Turpentine, mineral spirits, or other thinners may be used to alter the viscosity of the oil for better penetration. Boatbuilders working with unseasoned and green woods rely on this and similar mixtures to partially lessen the eventual splitting and cracking of big timbers. Woodcarvers find this a good solution in which to dip large carvings to retard splitting and checking. It leaves a heavy film on the surface, which further waterproofs the wood.

Oil also makes a stable sealing undercoat for varnish or paint. This helps the topcoat last longer, particularly on end grain where varnish or paint alone may not provide an effective seal. When varnishing over oil you must allow adequate drying time, two days at least and possibly weeks. Remove all dried oil deposits by scraping or sanding before varnishing. You may need to saturate with fresh oil and wipe immediately to soften and remove the crusted oils. A scraper works well to remove this crust.

Oils or Sealers?

In the last few years new products have appeared on the shelves, and old products have been repackaged. Two-part oil/sealer combinations have been developed that are more effective than oil alone. The array of products, each with its own claims, can be confusing even after a careful reading of the labeling, and finding the best product for each specific application may require some

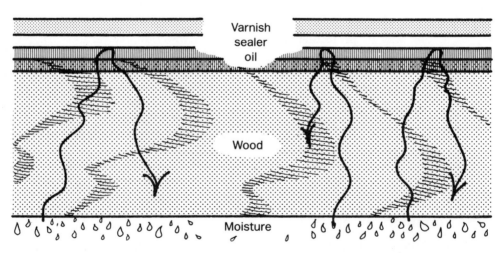

Sealer helps prevent lifting of varnish by moisture below.

research. When to use an oil, and when a sealer is more appropriate, can be difficult to decide, since their functions overlap somewhat.

As a general rule, oils tend to penetrate the surface more deeply and to darken the wood more than a sealer. They are usually petroleum-based. You can apply a sealer over an oil, but not vice versa, because the sealer would not allow effective penetration of an oil. Sealers, on the other hand, do not penetrate as well as oil; their function is surface sealing, to fill the pores on the wood surface. Sealers retain the original surface appearance of wood better than oil and can be removed by stripping the wood bare, whereas oil soaks into the wood. (The latter is only a problem if you try to paint directly over it with the wrong kind of paint.)

Neither a sealer nor an oil, used by itself, will stand up for much more than three months exposed to weather, and it won't last that long when used on exposed horizontal surfaces in hot climates. You can expect somewhat better performance when using oils and sealers in combination. Oil accomplishes deep penetration and stabilization of the wood, and the sealer provides an intermediate, or transitional, coating for varnish.

Oil isn't maintenance-free. If you want to keep it like new, you'll need to go over it again within two to four months, as you would with varnish. Application and maintenance is easier because oiling is easier than varnishing. Dust that would ruin a good varnish has little or no effect on an oiled surface. (Be sure to check the compatability of whatever oil you're using with seam or bedding compounds because oil may destroy their effectiveness.)

Oil Penetration

To improve penetration, the oil can be thinned and the wood can be warmed before and during application. A warm, sunny day is preferable for applying oil if you want the best penetration, and hand rubbing will help, since it generates heat and distributes the oil. Any thinners employed eventually will evaporate, leaving the oil in the wood.

Oak, in particular, and spruce are difficult to oil effectively without recurring problems of bleed-back (see next section). The cells are long and hollow, and trap pockets of air no matter how much effort you make to saturate and seal. Some finishers try to avoid oiling these woods because of this problem, but you may be able to accomplish more thorough saturation by warming the wood and the oil. If the piece is small enough to immerse in the oil, you can try heating them together, leaving the wood to cool overnight in the solution. As the wood cools it will draw oil deeper into the pores and accomplish a better seal.

Many amateur finishers try to achieve too smooth a finish and end up partially sealing the wood surface with fine sanding dust. For oiling, 100-grit is sufficient, and 80-grit is perfectly workable.

Oil Bleed-back

This is what occurs when spots of oil continue to return to the surface of oil-saturated wood, sometimes days after the surface has dried. The spots have a way of reappearing in the same location because of uneven or slash grain in that area. Since many hardwoods have tight uneven grains, it may happen in more than one location. It often occurs with oak because of the nature of the grain, but we've had the same problem with fine old air-dried Philippine mahogany, rosewood, teak, and yacal, as well as with softwoods. It's probably caused by air in the wood escaping and pushing the oil ahead of it, possibly in response to a change in atmospheric pressure, or by trapped moisture escaping as the wood warms. Whatever the reason, these little eruptions can upset your fine finish plans.

Most finishers learn to live with the problem, because no one seems to have a 100-percent workable solution. You can reduce the occurrence of bleed-back by drying and warming the wood before oiling, and doing so as far in advance as is practical. A

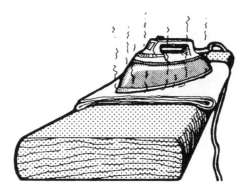

A hot iron applied over a damp towel and repeated as necessary helps prevent oil bleed-back.

wood-heated shop is best for this, and if you can leave wood in an overhead drying loft for as long as possible that may help. Choose a warm afternoon when the wood is warmed throughout, or a time after an extended spell of dry weather, which will have reduced the moisture content of the wood more than usual. Waiting as long as possible to begin final finishing after saturation oiling will also help. We once experimented with a warm iron, applied through a towel, to heat the surface of the wood where bleed-back had occurred, and this seemed to prevent further spotting in those areas.

You may get better saturation by allowing the wood to cool during preliminary oil-ing. Alternately warming and cooling the wood before final finishing may help by causing bleed-back to happen prematurely.

Wet Sanding With Oils

Some of the smoothest finishes attainable on hardwood come through using a wet sanding technique with oil. This treatment seems to work best on tight-grained hardwoods, but we've also used it on fir and spruce for interior cabinetry. This process involves flooding the wood with oil, paying particular attention to end grain. When maximum saturation is reached after three or four

Wet-sand repeatedly with oil and fine grit wet or dry sandpaper for a fine finish.

treatments, the surface is repeatedly wet-sanded using oil and 320- to 400-grit wet or dry sandpaper. The oil raises loose grain and the sanding cuts the grain flush with the surface, while the sanding dust mixes with the oil to form a very fine filler.

Hard hand sanding also creates heat, which aids penetration into the wood. For best results, warm the wood before oiling and sanding, and repeat the wet sanding operation four or five times, wiping down the wood *tight* and then letting it dry be-tween sandings. For interior cabinetry we use furniture wax over this surface for a mirror finish. The same technique can be used on exterior wood using varnish instead of wax.

Many oil formulations also contain a sunscreen ingredient that helps the surface to stay closer to the original color of the wood instead of bleaching from sunlight, and this sunscreen ingredient also helps the surface finish last longer.

Chapter Seven

Two-Part Polyurethanes

Two-part polyurethane paints introduced in the past few years have certainly upgraded boat finishing and refinishing. The new aliphatic urethanes provide higher gloss for longer periods of time and improve scuff and abrasion resistance; they also retain their original colors much longer than traditional paints. These paints are actually classed as coatings, not paint, because of their chemical makeup. "Two-part" refers to the two components that have to be mixed together at the time of application. Polyurethane is the generic name for the resin created by the two-part reaction. One-part polyurethanes are also available. They are pre-catalyzed in one container, but they fail to achieve the tenacity and colorfast quality of two-part mixtures.

When these high-tech formulations were first introduced, they required professional spray equipment and more experience than most amateur boat owners possessed. Many of these paints were developed for industrial and military applications, with emphasis on performance and efficiency without regard for amateur usage. They are expensive compared to traditional types. Most boat owners would think that paying $5,000 or more for a topside job on a 30-footer is outrageous, but if the paint lasts three to five times longer than traditional paints, it may be worth the money. Most of that bill — as much as 75 to 90 percent — is for labor, so you can enjoy great savings by doing the job yourself.

Many of the two-part paints can now be applied with roller and brush by any competent painter. Keep in mind, however, that the professional does it every day, has access to the best tools, and has already learned by his mistakes.

Hull Suitability

If the gelcoat of your fiberglass boat has become dull and chalky, two-part paint will take care of all that and give your boat more color than it probably had in the first place. Some paint manufacturers will even match your custom color sample, but it'll cost, so be sure to buy enough to finish the job the first time around.

An important consideration before buying and using these paints is whether or not your boat would look good with such a shiny finish. Keep in mind that a very high gloss will only highlight any flaws in the surface, so unless you're willing to do all the required preparation, spending the extra money may not be worthwhile. Often a much-used boat looks better with a flat or low-gloss paint job.

Whether or not it makes sense to use a two-part paint on a caulked plank-on-frame hull is debatable. If the seams are in good shape, small, and effectively caulked, then the high gloss of two-part paint might indeed improve the look of the hull (although many

A traditional wooden hull has seams that may be too flexible for certain coatings.

plank-on-frame hulls look just as good, if not better, with a flat paint). If you have to recaulk or maintain the seams every year, or even every three years, you should consider that two-part paint's effective lifespan of five to six years may be wasted. You may be better off with a more traditional yacht paint.

Cold-molded boats, since they're seamless and often sheathed with fiberglass cloth, can be considered in the same category as fiberglass boats as far as polyurethanes are concerned. Plywood hulls without seams are good candidates for high-quality paint jobs, and two-part paint will work well. Two-part polyurethane also works well on steel and aluminum, but again, the owner must make the decision as to whether the hull is fair enough to warrant a high-gloss paint job. Many metal hulls are not.

Surface Preparation

It's always wise to consult the manufacturer if there's any doubt about surface prepara-

tion when using these expensive paints. Expect about ten times the work in surface preparation and getting everything ready to paint as in the actual laying on of paint. Meticulous preparation is the key to success.

Although two-part polyurethanes can ostensibly be applied over a foundation of oil-based paints, you may still want to begin by stripping off the existing paint. It doesn't make any sense to apply expensive polyurethane over a flaky surface. The tenacious bond of the polyurethanes is established by strong solvents that etch and grip the surface, so if the surface isn't healthy in the first place, it should be removed.

If you doubt the condition of the old paint, but hate the thought of all that stripping, experiment with the old surface to see how sound it really is. Try a sample swatch of the two-part paint or just the thinner and see what happens. If the thinner supplied with the two-part paint in any way weakens, degrades, or lifts the old surface, you're back to plan A, complete stripping. If not, then on to plan B. You can possibly use a compatible primer or a transition coating as an undercoating for the two-part paint. Keep in mind that a primer coat should be well prepared before a high-gloss coating is applied, and plan to spend lots of time at it. Anything that's less than perfect will show up like a sore thumb after that high gloss is applied. Fill every tiny gouge and pore in the wood with an appropriate filler. We use epoxy and red or white microballoons for small filling jobs and a stronger structural filler such as silica, or a mixture of the two, on larger dents and gouges. For final sanding of the entire surface we use 220-grit paper, and for sanding between coats we go even finer. Do not use an oil-base tack cloth; instead, use a cloth saturated with the recommended thinner.

When preparing a fiberglass gelcoat surface for two-part paint, use the manufacturer's recommended solvent or cleaner. Fiberglass hulls, especially new ones, will retain mold release wax, and older fiberglass hulls will have remnants of cleaners and polishes that must all be removed. Always use solvent before you sand, and use it thoroughly. Scrub well and effectively, and finish one area before moving on.

Mixing and Thinning

In some cases paint sold over the counter to a boat owner is slightly different from the professional formulation and is usually an attempt by the manufacturer to make application technique less critical. Generally a different catalyst is supplied for brushing an otherwise professional sprayable mix to allow more time for rolling and brushing. If you're sure you want the professional formulation, you can find out about the proper application techniques by calling the manufacturer or talking to boatyards. They can fill you in on specific details of particular paints and recommended types of spray rigs.

Two-part polyurethanes must be mixed and thinned with care and strictly according to directions. If you choose not to mix the entire amount at one time, which is usually a very wise decision for a first-time polyurethane painter, you must meter out the exact amounts of both parts and mix them together without contaminating either container with its counterpart. We use a cup to dip from the can and pour into another measuring container, the contents of which are then poured into the mixing pot. Keep everything separated to avoid confusion. Begin a job with one person mixing and continue through to completion with the same mixer. All this may sound like unnecessary complication, but it actually simplifies the critical polyurethane mixing process, and if something goes wrong here, all the preparation in the world won't help.

Another time to employ a single mixer is when adding thinner. When the paint starts to drag on the brush or roller on a hot day or after working for a half hour or so, you'll need to add small amounts of thinner to allow proper flow and prevent leaving brush marks on the surface. A hot wind can make a very short "lap" time, and dark colors also warm much faster. Be careful to add thinner just a little at a time — too much, sometimes just a few drops too much, and the paint will run and drip. Start off with a few drops to a cup when mixing small amounts, get the feel of that, and a couple more as needed. It won't take much to achieve the proper viscosity, allowing the paint to flow just right. Sometimes you'll need to add thinner every few minutes, on a hot windy day, for example, and it becomes a challenge to keep the mixture just right. For best results, strive for a uniform coating and plan to do the recommended number of coats.

When two-part paint dries, the molecules cross-link giving this paint its longevity and tenacity, but the process can be slowed or even halted by freezing leftover portions of mixed paint. We have never tried this, but a friend freezes the leftovers at the end of a day (or whenever he wants to stop) and uses them later for touch-up. Keeping the paint cool and out of the sun when painting is another way to retard the chemical action and gain a longer working time.

Moisture and Two-Part Paint

Two-part polyurethanes react with the moisture in the air to achieve drying hardness, so you must keep an eye on the weather. Humidity of 40 to 60 percent is best; you can monitor the amount of moisture in the atmosphere with a hygrometer. In a closed and heated paint booth temperature and humidity can be controlled to a degree, but when you're working outside you're at the mercy of the elements. Horizontal surfaces in particular are very susceptible to moisture. About the best you can do is to choose the time of day and maybe turn the boat around to your advantage. In cold weather, you might turn a side to face the sun, or in hot weather, to face away from the sun. Although moisture in the air is necessary to achieve the proper reaction of the mixed paint, rain is a disaster, as are heavy dew, dust, and bugs settling on wet paint.

If sprayed, two-part paints are sensitive to contamination in the air lines and compressor, and we know of at least one job that blistered because of moisture in the lines. Filters can usually solve this problem.

Roller and Brush Application

If you're using a roller and brush, buy high-quality rollers and brushes. It's surprising how often we've seen a boat owner spend $40 for a quart of paint and try to slap it on with a 39-cent brush. Sometimes you get away with it, sometimes you don't, but the result is seldom the best finish.

Remember that two-part urethanes are potent and highly toxic chemicals. Adhere strictly to the safety precautions described in Chapter 1. Proper ventilation is essential.

Foam rubber rollers provide better control of paint than other types and are still inexpensive enough to discard after each use. Each paint manufacturer has its own recommended rollers and brushes, and we can vouch for the fact that it's wise to listen and follow that advice. These materials are not expensive, relative to accomplishing a fine paint job; buy plenty of them before you start mixing. There are strong solvents in the paint, so if a roller starts to leave bits of itself on the surface or to delaminate, or if its surface starts to wrinkle, replace it with a new one. We like to have a couple of fresh rollers within reach, already mounted on clean handles.

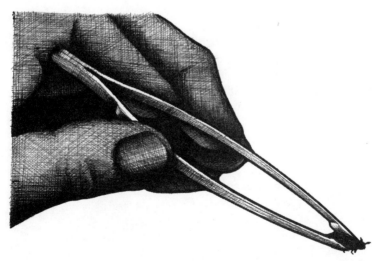

Remove bristles and kamikaze bugs from your work area with tweezers.

Rollers
cut easily
with a
sharp knife

Keep plenty of foam rollers cut and ready to use, as well as extra handles.

We often use a roller to spread the paint on the surface as uniformly as possible, because a roller will hold more paint than a brush and make a wider swath; we then follow up with a careful brushing. Use the best, most comfortable brush you can find to do the final brushing. Check to ensure that the brush bristles are compatible with the solvents in the paint. Some synthetic bristle may not survive the solvents for very long. You can experiment with a small test patch to see how the bristle fares, or else check with the manufacturer (of either the brush or the paint) for specific recommendations. We normally use the roller to apply the paint in one direction, across the grain on wood, then brush with the grain for a smoother finish and the least visible brush marks. On fiberglass topsides we always finish brush with horizontal strokes, parallel to the waterline and the sheer of the hull.

Work in small sections, even after you're familiar with the paint. If you're rolling paint on ahead of a partner, don't get too far ahead of the brush, even with the best of conditions, and keep good brush technique in mind. Putting the brush on the surface to start a stroke leaves a mark, whereas lifting off does not — at least if you've thinned according to directions. If the paint is too thick and pulling or dragging on the brush, you may leave marks regardless and also end up with slow-motion sags. Plan a pattern of brush strokes that will cover your "put-down," such as a final stroking backwards

Test first to be sure your brush bristle type is compatible with the solvents in your paint!

Roll against the grain first, then brush with the grain.

to your direction of progress. We have a favorite 2½-inch brush that we keep especially for polyurethanes, and that width is just right for smaller areas. A 3-inch or 4-inch brush is good on a topside with extensive acreage to cover.

A tip for using rollers: Foam rollers may be cut to specific widths on a band saw or with a sharp clean handsaw or knife to make it easier to work in small areas and when cutting in with the roller. This technique, a short roller on a small handle, is effective when you paint a boottop or sheer stripe between strips of masking tape.

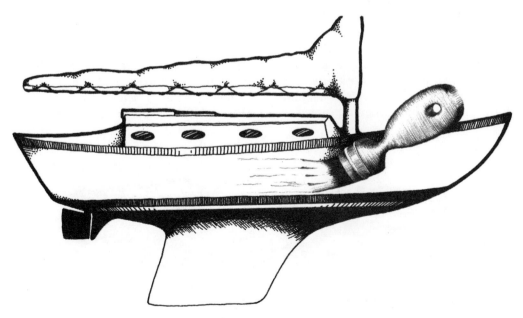

On fiberglass hulls, brush parallel with the sheer and waterline.

Chapter Eight

Sealants and Caulkings

Not too long ago, a boatbuilder's choice of sealants and caulking materials was limited to linseed oil, heavy felt, antifungicidal compound, red lead, or combinations of these things. Caulkings were mostly oakum with its nostalgic smell, or for smaller seams, twisted strands of cotton tapped into place with a caulking iron and mallet. The success of the job usually depended on the experience level of the caulker. Good caulkers always seemed to have work, and work it was, slow and backbreaking, leaning all the time or working overhead. If the seam gaped and the planking had shrunk, chances were good that the hull would eventually "spit" her caulking and then leak. About the best you could do was dab some thick paint into the seam to try to hold everything in place. You could have plenty of work trying to caulk up a wracked old hull with all her hundreds of yards of seams. Strict traditionalists

continue in this manner, but there are a number of alternatives now available.

Polysulphides

Polysulphide caulking, in the now-familiar cartridge tubes that fit caulking guns, has been around for quite a number of years and was probably the first type of caulking sealant to enjoy widespread use on boats. For years, we relied on it for a variety of caulking and general waterproofing functions, and it always did a decent job.

A 30-foot fiberglass hull might take as many as three dozen tubes by the time the hull-to-deck clamp connection was made, the teak decks were laid over the fiberglass, and the portholes and hardware were bedded. After a while, the polysulphide would stiffen slightly, and it never had the

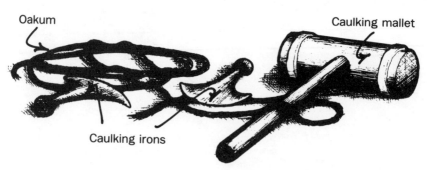

Oakum

Caulking mallet

Caulking irons

The tools of the trade for traditional caulking.

72

Caulking gun and caulking compound.

remarkable adhesion of polyurethanes or silicone, but it did and still does a passable job. It's usually the least expensive of the available caulking materials, although some of the new acrylics are now comparably priced.

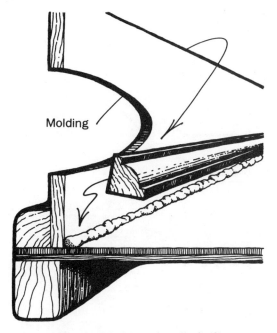

A molding bedded in a bead of silicone.

Molding

Polyurethanes

Polyurethanes provide a faster curing time, better adhesion, and longer lasting flexibility than polysulphides. It takes them two to four days to set up to full strength, but they're tack-free in a matter of hours (sometimes minutes), which makes them cleaner to use aboard a busy boat. They stick a lot more tenaciously than polysulphides, and they stick to just about anything — including your clothes and teak decks if you're not careful. Moldings and other pieces become structural when attached with these high-strength beddings. Polyurethane can be painted over; it is also available in colors to match wood and trim. Because they are effective bonding agents, you may not want to use either polyurethane or silicone on anything that has to be periodically removed.

Silicone

Silicone seal has more uses aboard a boat than a bucket: not only for routine (and emergency) caulking but as a glue, a seam filler, and gasket material. Small boats can be virtually rebuilt with silicone seal. I carry a tube of it and a roll of duct tape in my sea kayak, and with these two items I can cope with just about any damage. It's great for mounting small pieces of hardware that need bedding and bonding at the same time. If you doubt the tenacity of silicone seal, stick two pieces of scrap plywood together with it, wait a few days, and try to take them apart — you'll need a hammer and chisel. We've used silicone alone to hold small windowpanes in place. Most people don't have much success painting over silicone because it's so flexible that it cracks the paint.

You can sometimes find silicone seal in black, which is good for gaskets; it's also commonly available in white and gray to match surrounding trim. Although colored silicone will resist the harmful effects of sunlight a little better than clear, the clear silicone forms an opaque film over the surface that also affords some protection from the elements. If you cut into an old bead of

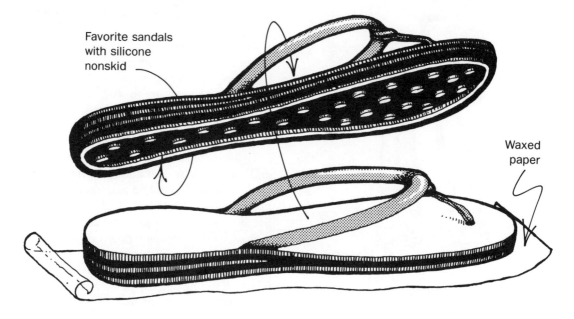

Favorite sandals
with silicone
nonskid

Waxed
paper

silicone that has not been exposed to strong bleaches or solvents, you'll find it's still lively and flexible and doing the job. Silicone seems to retain its good bond for years and will do so even when placed against wood that has later rotted or been watersoaked. It will also establish a good bond on metal.

Whether or not silicone should be used below the waterline is debatable; manufacturers don't recommend doing so, but I know of a number of instances in which it has been used there with success. It's best for temporary or emergency repairs.

You can use silicone to make very effec-

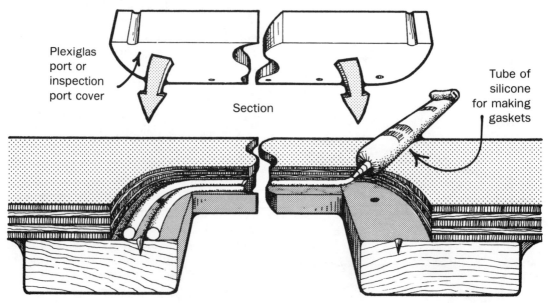

Plexiglas
port or
inspection
port cover

Section

Tube of
silicone
for making
gaskets

To make a port removable, use waxed paper between Plexiglas and silicone, and fasten lightly. Remove waxed paper after silicone has kicked, and replace the port.

tive gaskets in just about any shape. Place waxed paper on both sides of the silicone and apply a steady source of pressure against it until the silicone has cured for awhile. Then remove the waxed paper, and you'll have a perfect gasket. Use scissors to trim as necessary.

With a little practice, you can also form pleasing, cove-shaped fillets of silicone rubber. We wear surgical gloves and form them with thumb and forefinger, which is just about the right radius for pleasing contours around moldings, winch pads, and portholes. They make a fine moisture seal and look good, particularly in colors. To make a finger fillet, start forming it as soon as you lay a bead from the tube. Silicone will start to "skin" over as soon as it's exposed to the air, and you must form the fillet before this happens. The fumes are strong until it skins over, and be careful not to rub silicone around your eyes.

If you're shopping for tubes of silicone seal, be sure you're getting the real thing. We sometimes run across bargain bin specials of tubes marked "silicone" that are actually a silicone/acrylic mixture, or something else; these sealants never seem to perform as well as the real thing. If you're in doubt, buy a tube and try it. If it works, go back and buy as much as you need.

Epoxy Beddings

Epoxy can also be used to produce a moderately flexible, high-strength bedding that is impervious to water. Mix epoxy resin with a filler such as microballoons, trowel it into place, then position the hardware and tighten down. The epoxy will cure in place and form a very tough bond. The bedding will not have anywhere near the flexibility of silicone or polyurethane, but it will be much stronger and more flexible than many other glues. This is an ideal high-strength, waterproof, and form-fitting bedding for winch pads and other hardware; it will adhere to wood, fiberglass, and even metals.

Working with Caulk

Make sure you get fresh caulking; avoid old tubes from a carton that's sat around for years. Shelf life can be affected by freezing, and although we've used tubes that have

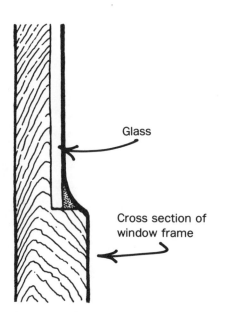

Glass

Cross section of
window frame

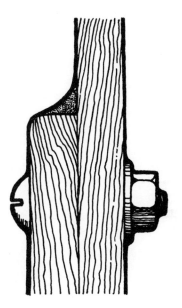

Examples of filleting with silicone.

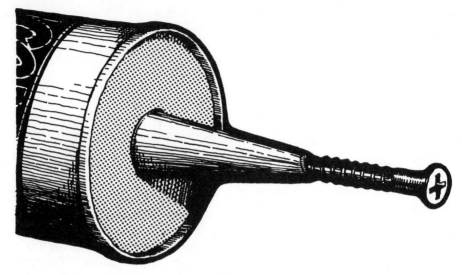

A wood screw in an opened cartridge tip can help save a tube of silicone.

been frozen without any apparent problems, it's not recommended.

Wipe up spills as soon as possible, using an appropriate mild solvent. Caulk is tough to remove once it hardens in the pores of the wood. It will leave a mark on paint, and it's also very difficult to remove from nonskid fiberglass gelcoat decking.

Think before you cut off the end of a new tube. Unless you want to squeeze out as much caulk as possible in a hurry, a small slanting cut at the end of the tip will allow the best control. Remember that tempera-ture will affect the rate of flow from the tube, and adjust the size of your cut accordingly; on colder days caulk is like molasses, and on hot days it may almost drip out in a puddle, even from a very small opening.

If you don't use up the entire cartridge, you'll need to seal the tip to keep air from the remaining caulk. We prefer to fill the spout with a large screw. When it's removed later, probably with pliers, the threads will pull out any silicone that may have cured in the spout.

Chapter Nine

Masts and Spars

The masts and spars atop most modern sailboats are made of aluminum, but wooden spars can be found on fiberglass, steel, or aluminum boats, as well as on plank-on-frame classics and new wooden boats. As technology and production techniques improve, composite spars of carbon fiber and other petrochemical-derived materials may become more popular. Whatever the material, masts and spars can benefit from some level of finish.

Aluminum Masts and Spars

Aluminum will last quite a while without care of any kind, which is one of its primary attractions. It is not, however, maintenance-free, at least not if you want it to maintain full strength and continue to look good. Aluminum left untreated will oxidize, forming a protective crust that will partially weatherproof the surface, but left alone it will suffer eventual damage in the form of pitting and corrosion. Rivets and fastenings of dissimilar alloys may also cause mild electrolysis to weaken critical areas. If an aluminum mast has been neglected for years, it might be wise to have a professional inspect it for basic soundness before you undertake extensive repair and finishing. A giveaway to the true condition of the mast is usually in the fittings — tangs, cleats, spreaders, sail track, and so on. Many of

these are riveted, which traps salt and dirt, forming pockets of corrosion. We've seen some very neglected and abused masts brought back by stripping and refinishing, but they should be carefully inspected.

Aside from leaving aluminum bare to fend for itself, or waxing, which is a temporary measure at best, the two prevalent choices are to anodize or to paint. Cleaning and waxing will maintain an aluminum mast in decent condition for a while — six months or so if fastidiously applied for the first time — at least long enough to decide on the next type of treatment. Even meticulous cleaning and waxing on a regular schedule is a second choice to anodizing or painting, which offer real and lasting protection.

A good scrubbing with bronze wool will remove oxidation from bare aluminum, and application of wax will delay the weathering process for a few months in mild climates, but it must be done regularly and completely, paying particular attention to rivets, attachments and fastenings, and crevices where salt and corrosion accumulate. Thorough cleaning of a mast is a considerable task and may require the use of small brushes, scrapers and other tools. If the metal has already pitted from exposure, 600-grit paper will smooth the surface somewhat and get back to bare metal, but bear in mind that such pitting weakens a thin-walled aluminum section.

Anodizing is an electro-chemical process

that coats the mast with aluminum oxide, and can be done in either a hard or soft mode. Hard-anodizing produces a longer-lasting finish that can also be painted over, giving even more protection. In order to anodize you must remove the mast, strip it of all fittings, and transport it to a facility equipped to do the job. A good hard-anodizing will usually last four to six years if you're careful with the mast. Anodizing will chip and scrape from rough treatment and should be patched with paint in those places. Anodized aluminum retains its strength and health even though the surface is less than perfect, and it can be maintained by thorough cleaning and rinsing and the application of protective formulations, such as paint.

Paint is itself a good protection for masts and spars, and one that can be applied by the boat owner himself. A high-quality paint, such as a two-part polyurethane, may last even longer than anodizing. All the established rules of good painting apply, including meticulous surface preparation, as outlined in Chapter 7.

Before you paint aluminum, you must remove oxidation and any wax buildup that may have accumulated. After a thorough cleaning, scrub the mast with bronze wool and then sand with 600-grit sandpaper, working lengthwise along the mast. You can use a water test to determine if the metal is clean and ready for paint. Wipe the mast with a wet sponge: any areas not cleaned to bare metal will bead, and these spots can be marked for further cleaning.

The type of paint you choose will determine the correct primer, so be sure to consult the manufacturer's instructions. An alternative to primer is epoxy resin, which pro-

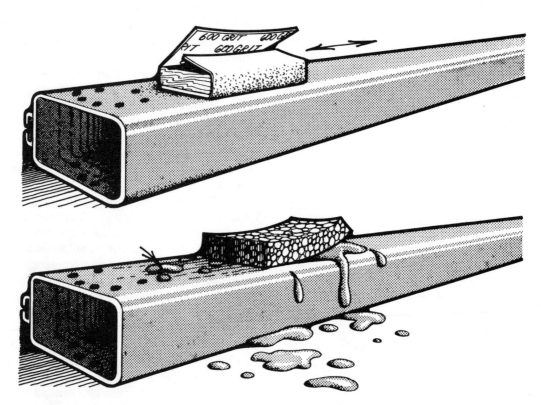

Before aluminum is painted, all wax and oxidation must be removed. Scrub with bronze wool; final sand with 600-grit paper. A water test will determine if the metal is clean and ready for paint. Beads of water mean area needs more cleaning.

vides an effective, flexible, and tenacious undercoat or "tie" coating for aluminum masts, over which paint may be applied. We have used an epoxy undercoat successfully on aluminum masts by following the manufacturer's instructions carefully and by using an etching solution on the metal to ensure a good bond. An acid etch isn't necessary for paint because sanding will usually provide a sufficient base.

Even with a brushable polyurethane and the finest brush, you may leave brush marks, but keep in mind that once the mast is stepped in the boat, you seldom see tiny mistakes much higher than eye level, anyway! It might be best to start at the masthead, and perfect your brushing technique before you get to the more visible butt end of the mast.

Wooden Masts and Spars

Wood needs more care than metal, and should never be left bare. Glue lines, feathered scarph ends, and hardware attachments need a positive moisture seal for long and healthy life. Hollow masts, booms and yards may need a seal inside as well as outside. If water is allowed into a hollow spar through masthead fittings, cable entries, or hardware attachments, it becomes an ideal environment for rot. A hollow wood mast needs to be sealed before and during glue-up. For obvious reasons, it is impractical to try to seal the inside of a completed mast. Well-designed masts still provide a drain hole at the step, but all fittings must be well sealed to prevent pockets of rot.

Varnish is a good traditional treatment for wooden spars, and is still the most widely used. A finely crafted spruce or fir mast looks elegant with a half-dozen coats of spar varnish. It's hard to imagine painting a piece that complements a well-kept boat, but many masts and spars are eventually painted because the owner is simply tired of the extra effort involved in maintaining a clear finish.

Sheathing Masts and Spars

For a natural finish on masts, plus an additional degree of protection and stiffening, sheathing with fiberglass cloth and epoxy is effective and long-lasting. (Refer to Chapter 5 for more information.) Epoxy is flexible enough to bend with the wood, even on springy, unstayed masts. Sheathing is not a viable option if you use polyester or vinylester resins.

A notable complication to sheathing is that masts and spars, because of their long and narrow shape, require more preparation and forethought. Very seldom will you be able to sheathe an entire mast in one operation. It usually requires at least two steps — you do half or three-quarters of the cir-

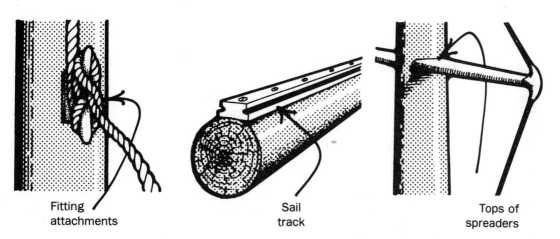

| Fitting attachments | Sail track | Tops of spreaders |

Vulnerable rot spots on masts and spars.

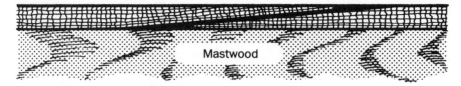

A fiberglass joint lapped and feather-edged.

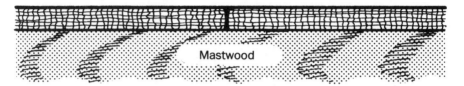

A fiberglass butt joint.

cumference of the mast on the first operation; then, when the epoxy has kicked, you roll the mast over, feather the edge, and finish the job. A sharp block plane, rasp, file, and sanding blocks will produce an almost invisible feather edge. Unless you want extra buildup, a 1-inch overlap is sufficient — even a butt joint is acceptable. Arrange the overlaps of joints on the least-seen sides if you don't like the joint's appearance. It can be put under the sail track on center line aft, or port and starboard.

Sheathing is also a particularly good treatment for specific areas of masts that suffer abrasion from gaff jaws, mast hoops, battens in a Chinese rig, and sail-control lines that chafe. The only problem is that you have to plan ahead and sheathe before the mast is oiled or painted. You may be able to take a painted mast down to bare wood and effectively sheathe, but an oiled mast, because of oil penetration, will never accept epoxy properly — although epoxy will stick better than anything else.

Normally we use 4-ounce E-type cloth for lighter masts and spars and 6-ounce for a bit more strength and durability. You'll be able to see the cloth in places, just barely, but if you presaturate the wood well with epoxy resin, there should be nothing worse than slight opacity. If you're planning to paint the mast and you just want the most protection in a stabilizing, strength-

enhancing undercoating, then 7½-ounce cloth or even 9-ounce might be appropriate. Keep in mind that you'll be adding considerable weight to the mast when you use heavier cloth or layers of cloth because it takes more epoxy resin to saturate it. We added 21 pounds to a 40-foot Sitka spruce mast. The mast was unstayed and had a diameter of almost 11 inches at the partners, tapering to 4½ inches at the masthead, so there was considerably more area than with a slimmer, stayed mast. We used 6-ounce cloth with overlaps to port and starboard.

On a 15-foot by 3-inch-diameter spruce yard, which we sheathed with 4-ounce cloth, we added just over 3 pounds. Four-ounce cloth will add less than half the weight of 6-ounce cloth because the cloth is much lighter and requires much less resin to saturate it. Heavier cloth, 7½-ounce, for example, requires still more resin and can almost double the weight of a 6-ounce layup. Anyone who contemplates sheathing spars should inspect samples of the various weights and experiment to find the best for each situation.

Precut fiberglass tape in appropriate widths eases the job of sheathing a long narrow piece. The bound selvage edge is neater to work with and provides a more definite edge than cutting a strip of cloth from a roll. Another advantage of fiberglass tape is that you can roll it on in one continuous length,

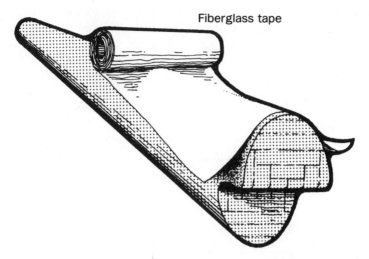

Fiberglass tape

Fiberglass tape makes for much easier and cleaner work to sheathe one-half to three-quarters of a mast at one time. After the first run kicks, feather-edge and sheathe the remaining one-quarter to one-half of the mast with the same width or narrower tape.

then pull on the ends to align and position the tape, something you may not be able to accomplish with rough-cut cloth. The selvage edge of the tape will saturate uniformly and not leave tiny sharp *hairs* of fiberglass sticking up. Tape is easier to wrap around a corner, and if you must end on an edge or corner of a mast, then it will lay down better. If you get a tiny edge curl, leave it until it cures, then slice it off clean with a sharp plane and fill with epoxy.

Support any mast so it is perfectly straight and level before you sheathe. Fiberglass and epoxy add a lot of stiffness,

and if the mast isn't straight you may glass in a "wow." On the other hand, you can also take unwanted shape out of small, lighter masts by sheathing them with a prearranged curve. Sometimes sheathing is used just to reinforce a mast and may be applied over or with graphite or unidirectional glass fibers.

One easy way to arrange supports for a mast about to be sheathed, without building a spar bench, is the use of sawhorses with scraps of plywood and clamps. Arrange the horses at sufficient intervals according to the size of the mast and clamp on scraps of plywood to make a flat bed. Use the clamps

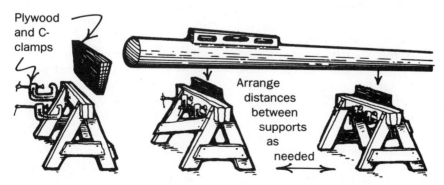

Plywood and C-clamps

Arrange distances between supports as needed

Adjustable supports make a level temporary bench for sheathing masts and spars.

to adjust the ply supports to make them level, then screw them into place. Long, skinny stayed masts are quite limber and should be supported every three or four feet.

Sheathing can also be done while the mast is still vertical in the boat, but you will have to do one short section at a time. Sheathing in place works best for repair or small areas that need reinforcement or protection and usually requires presaturating the glass cloth and carrying it aloft.

Refinishing a Mast on the Ground

Given the option, almost anyone with experience would choose to unstep and remove a mast from the boat for refinishing. In terms of effort expended, removing the rigging is usually more efficient than going up and down the mast and working in a bosun's chair, and the end result is usually a better job.

Even when you get the mast off the boat and level on sawhorses, you'll still have tactical difficulties. If the mast is a round-sectioned one, you must decide whether to try to cover the entire circumference with each successive coat; or to do half, or three-quarters, of the circumference, then roll the mast over and do the rest. A rectangular or square-sectioned mast is easier because it offers defined points at which to stop and feather the edge for successive coats. You can usually arrange by proper bracing to do three-quarters of a mast circumference, whether round or rectangular in section, then roll it for the remaining one-quarter.

The supports, depending on the weight and size of the mast, can be blocks of wood with plastic over them, or wedge-shaped pieces, and they must be clean and dry. You may be able to support the mast along its length with small, strategically placed blocks enabling you to reach under and do the entire circumference the first time through, leaving only small spots where the support pads were located. You can finish those later, perhaps when the mast is stepped in the boat. A sturdy 30-foot mast may, for instance, be supported at each end and with only two or three supports in the middle,

which will make it feasible to use this method. Be sure to wedge the mast securely in place so it doesn't roll off the supports. Very often, especially when working with smaller masts, you can hang the stick from the overhead by the fittings. For a first-class job, remove all detachable fittings, and then inspect and rebed them. You should be able to do this at the sanding stage. Then hang the mast from the masthead fitting, spreaders, tangs and cleats, or whatever is available. Each situation demands a slightly different approach depending on the size and condition of the mast and the facilities available.

Refinishing a Mast On The Boat

Although we ourselves prefer to unstep a mast before working on it, many owners choose to refinish their mast in place on the boat. Booms, yards, and other spars can still be removed and laid flat for refinishing, and there are techniques that can help reduce the hassles — and hazards — of working aloft.

If you own a ketch, schooner, or three-masted barkentine you could easily spend two or three weeks a year in a bosun's chair maintaining the masts. Get yourself a comfortable and safe bosun's chair — not just a ladder rung on a halyard, but a canvas envelope with high back and sides that will cradle you like a baby bird in a nest and make you feel as secure as possible. You may need to insert some kind of stiffener in the bottom of the fabric envelope to keep it from pinching or cutting off circulation. Most people are uncomfortable enough at mast-top altitudes, and anything to improve concentration will be beneficial to the finished job. The most comfortable apparatus we ever saw was a small fiberglass bucket seat roped into a canvas envelope and equipped with D rings for hoisting.

Figure out some efficient way to carry all the tools you'll need (see illustration) because trips up and down take time and effort and sending tools up and down on a messenger line isn't the answer. Try not to drop anything because whatever falls will ding your deck, get lost in the water, or bang

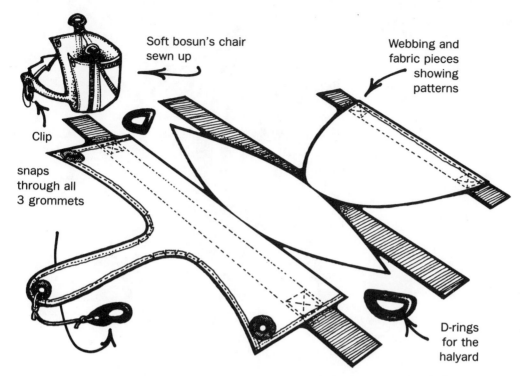

Soft bosun's chair sewn up

Webbing and fabric pieces showing patterns

Clip

snaps through all 3 grommets

D-rings for the halyard

You can make your own sturdy bosun's chair for journeys aloft.

someone on the head. A rigging knife or a paint can falling from the sky is not amusing to close neighbors or those in the cone of danger under a masthead.

Get everything out of the way. Take off spare halyards and lines, and secure them with duct tape or shock cord somewhere so they can't flap against the mast. A loose halyard in the wind makes interesting snake-track patterns in wet paint or varnish.

You'll need a winch helper — someone who won't take off in the middle of the job and leave you stranded, and whom you trust to handle the lifting winch. The first few times up and down, wrap your legs loosely around the mast as a safety precaution. Later on in the job you won't be able to, but it will help you gain confidence at first, in both yourself and your winch handler.

Our neighbors at one marina rigged a counterweight to assist the lifting operation, since they were up and down the mast any number of times over a two-week period. They filled first one, then a second 5-gallon jug with water, clipped them to the forestay with a carabiner, and fastened the end of the halyard to the bosun's chair. The weight of

the water provided some counterweight to make lifting and lowering easier. This is not a bad idea if you're tied securely to the docks and plan on going up and down a number of times. Tie or clip off the chair when you come down for a break so the jugs don't crash to the deck!

Plan your up and down trips to make them productive each time. Your winch helper will appreciate it. For instance, inspect and remove hardware on the way up, sand down, clean dust and tack cloth up, seal and varnish down, and so on. If it's a long spar you might wish to finish the top half or third, complete the entire finishing operation in panels and move down. You may eventually feel more comfortable about heights that way. Climbing and working on a tall mast is an adrenalin-provoking experience for someone who doesn't do it all the time. After working atop a 40-foot mast for half a day, I couldn't get to sleep at night. After working on a 50-footer, the 40-foot mast seemed tame. Keep in mind however, that you can suffer real injury from even a 4-foot fall.

Once I climbed a 40-foot mast while the

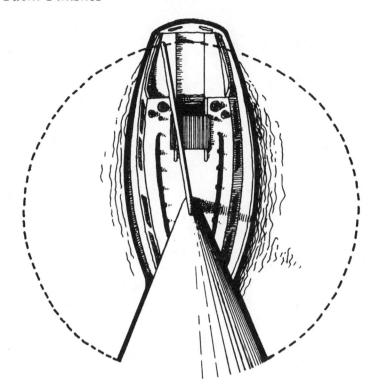

The "cone of danger" while working atop a masthead.

boat was anchored in a cove with a very slight swell running, and my fingerprints are, I'm sure, still embedded all around the masthead. It's a good idea to tie stiffly up to a sheltered dock, since every ripple is magnified into a swing at the masthead. You simply can't do quality work while hanging on in terror.

Before you go aloft, try to get everything out from under the mast, away from the danger zone, which extends downward in a cone around the base of the mast. Warn the neighbors in the next slip and take the polite precaution of covering each of their boats with a drop cloth. Have your winch handler run the lifting halyard through a turning block and aft to a cockpit winch, if possible, instead of working right under the mast. By moving away from the mast, your helper will have a better view of you aloft and can anticipate your needs.

Clip bags for tools onto the bosun's chair. Put paint and varnish cans in a bucket

Short loop of line with caribiner snaps counterweight onto forestay

Line runs to masthead and down to bosun's chair

A 5-gallon jug of water makes a good counterweight to help when going up the mast.

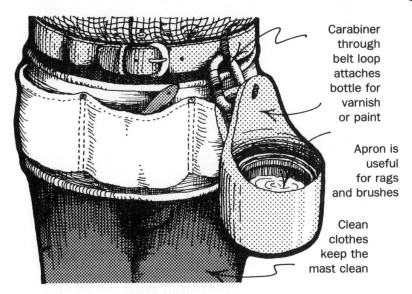

Carabiner through belt loop attaches bottle for varnish or paint

Apron is useful for rags and brushes

Clean clothes keep the mast clean

A well-planned kit for journeys aloft.

or a plastic bleach bottle with the top cut away and the handle left in place for the clip. This will catch drips, and prevent an even more disastrous full-scale spill in a gust of wind. It will also provide a tiny windbreak as you wet the brush. Move slowly while you're aloft and be sure of your actions. Some people get dizzy at heights; if you do, put your tools in the bag and hug the mast for awhile. If you're taking an electric tool aloft, tie knots in the extension cords so they won't come apart when you pull up. Always keep in mind that the wind will blow paint drops and dust some distance from the mast. Wind is a problem when you're aloft, and if it blows hard you'll have to leave the job till later.

As a matter of good varnishing technique, don't leave bare wood on the mast for any length of time. If you have to abandon the job before you finish, try to brush on a quick coat of sealer or thinned varnish, something to protect the wood. Anything left overnight must be cleaned before you start to varnish, to remove dust or salt from a seabreeze. In order to keep the mast clean, change out of your sanding overalls before you go up to varnish, and don't wear greasy clothes.

Larger spars have more area, and that means wider brushes; a 1½-inch brush is our choice for most 30- to 40-foot masts. Smaller spars may require smaller brushes, especially for cutting in and getting close to tangs, spreaders and the sail track. On most trips to the masthead I try to take along an extra small brush just for cutting in around hardware, since this is the measure of a good job and also the first place an owner will look when inspecting the job. These difficult areas may also require chisels and scrapers for cleaning before final varnish. Again, it's always better to remove the hardware if at all possible and do a proper job, than to work around something that may hide problems underneath. Anytime there's a question about the health of a certain fastening, remove the piece and bed it with the appropriate compound, caulking, or epoxy. Epoxy is the best choice for blackened wood around fastenings in the sail track. If the wood is still sound, insert a few drops of epoxy in the screw or bolt hole, using a small acid brush, dip the fastening and replace it. Use a new screw if necessary and do the same for any through bolts that appear to be degrading the wood by condensation of moisture or leaching salts into the wood.

Chapter Ten

Decks

Laid Decks

Before plywood was finally accepted as a proper boatbuilding material, timber decks had to provide both structural stability and watertightness. How well they did this, and for how long, depended on the quality of the timber and the skill of the shipwright and the caulkers. Leaks were a fact of life at sea because the many pieces required to build and reinforce a deck provided hundreds of yards of seams through which water could eventually find its way. These leaks, especially those from the rain, provided multiple opportunities for pockets of rot. Laid wooden decks are still popular, but nowadays, except on strictly traditional boats, they are usually fastened over fiberglass or plywood. Traditional wooden decks can be applied to all types of hulls, including steel, ferrocement, and aluminum.

Decking strips of teak or cedar are usually bedded, fastened, and caulked from above. Modern bedding compounds have partly solved the problem of rot between the layers of decking. Laid wooden decks are popular over fiberglass decks, where they are bedded and fastened to the glass with self-tapping screws. They can also be glued with epoxy, in which case no other permanent fastenings are needed, and screws may be removed when the epoxy kicks.

After the deck is installed and all fastening holes are plugged, deck caulking is nor-

mally applied between the strips. This caulking can be purchased from a number of suppliers, the best type being a two-part polysulphide polymer mix applied with a caulking gun. The seams between decking strips are filled slightly above the surface with caulking; after it sets overnight, the builder sands the deck with a belt sander, which brings the caulking flush with the top of the wood. Good caulking compound will maintain a watertight bond with the wood strips on either side and will adjust to expansion or contraction by bulging or shrinking slightly above or below the decking surface. This elasticity or frequent movement of a laid wooden deck is the reason a flexible caulking is necessary.

Laid wooden decks provide a reasonably good nonskid surface. They may be left natural, and when cleaned regularly and scrubbed with a stiff brush they develop small grooves where the wood wears away, enhancing the nonskid characteristics of the surface. Some finishers choose to oil or seal the wooden deck for additional protection, aiming at a good compromise between protection and a nonskid surface. Oil will keep the wood healthy longer, but will probably require more cleaning because it retains dust and dirt. Boiled linseed oil, perhaps thinned with kerosene or mixed with stain if desired, is appropriate for this purpose. Linseed oil with additives is available under various proprietary names. Some owners treat wooden

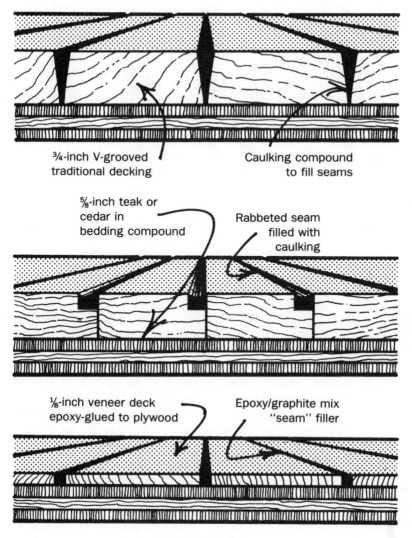

¾-inch V-grooved
traditional decking

Caulking compound
to fill seams

⅝-inch teak or
cedar in
bedding compound

Rabbeted seam
filled with
caulking

⅛-inch veneer deck
epoxy-glued to plywood

Epoxy/graphite mix
"seam" filler

Decking types.

decks with a thinned varnish, which offers good penetration and some protection to the wood without the buildup of a number of coatings. Such a finish will not become as slick as one might imagine. More than a few coats of thinned varnish will, however, make a deck very slick. Varnish will also not last very long on a caulked deck because each seam of caulking will expand and contract, providing an entry for moisture.

Deck strips are usually either V-grooved or rabbeted. The strips are laid fore and aft, parallel with the centerline of the boat, or wrapped gracefully around the cabin sides and the sheer of the hull. V-grooved seams

were formerly cotton-caulked, leaving just ¼-inch depth on top into which the rubberized caulking was applied. The effectiveness of modern caulkings, however, has eliminated the need for cotton-caulking the seams. Filling the entire seam with rubberized deck caulk seals the wood better, lasts longer, and eliminates much of the potential for rot if and when moisture gets into the bottom of the seam.

Reefing Old Deck Seams

Laid decking strips that are still in fair shape, with no rot or unusual wear, are good candidates for recaulking, which can seal the

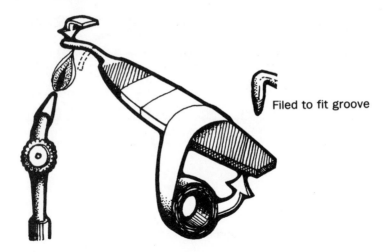

Filed to fit groove

To make a reefing tool heat file handle tip and bend it to a 90-degree angle, then file the tip to fit the groove in the deck. Tape the handle for a good grip.

deck and renew its appearance. The process of removing old caulk is known as reefing. A good method for doing this is to make a reefing tool from an old file or screwdriver. The end is heated and bent 90 degrees, then sharpened and filed to fit the caulking groove, whether V-shaped or flat-bottomed. When the hook is pulled lengthwise along the seam, it will reef (or ''reeve'') out the old caulking. Be particularly attentive to getting the crusty, ''dead'' caulk out of the seam sides, so the new application will adhere to the wood. Scraping or shaving with a sharp chisel works well. Electric tools may be adapted for cleaning these seams, but unless you have a large area of deck and are competent with power tools, a router or circular saw can do a lot of damage. It's hard to injure a deck with a hand tool.

After all the old caulk is removed, vacuum the seams, inspecting and scraping each one. In most cases a caulk primer will improve adhesion. Caulk primer is available from caulk distributors; follow manufacturers' recommendations to select a primer for the caulk you are using.

Sanded Decks

A *sanded* deck, in this case, doesn't mean that you rub it with sandpaper; it means that you apply clean, dry sand over the surface of a newly painted deck to improve its grip. Sanding is a tried-and-true method of providing a positive nonskid surface. A sanded deck will scrape skin right off watersoaked knees and knuckles and chafe right through foul-weather gear, but it provides as good as you're going to get for adhesion.

Sand can be applied over the entire deck or just along walkways. It can also be applied to selected high-use spots where adhesion is needed for safety and efficiency, such as where you place your feet while working a winch or hauling an anchor. The rest of the deck can be left gelcoated or smooth.

Sanding will work on fiberglass, plywood, canvas, steel, aluminum, or ferrocement — just about any surface that can be painted. (In the case of aluminum, use epoxy resin to glue sand to a clean, etched surface; then paint it.) Sand can be procured in buckets from a local beach or riverbed, but since it must be graded, strained, and washed, we usually just buy a bag of washed sand from a masonry or building supply house. Make a sand shaker from a coffee can by punching small holes in the bottom.

Mask off the area you wish to sand, prepare the surface properly, and apply a generous coating of paint. While the paint is still wet, shake on a heavy layer of washed

A soup can sand shaker for "sanding" decks.

sand. The next step is important in achieving a long-lasting sanding job: After the paint has dried for a day or so, carefully vacuum or sweep off the excess loose sand and then brush or roll a coating of paint over the surface. Let the sand set as long as possible without disturbing it. Leave it alone for up to a week if possible, which will allow the paint to season and attain the hardness it needs to hold the grains of sand.

Regular marine alkyd enamel paints are often used for this purpose, particularly on wood and canvas-covered wood decks; the treatment will need to be renewed as often as once a year, and for a wooden boat this becomes one more item on the spring commissioning agenda. Eventually the overall buildup of paint, which will lose its adhesion and begin lifting and flaking in spots, will necessitate scraping down to the bare surface and beginning anew.

A more long-lasting treatment, particularly on dimensionally stable fiberglass decks, is to use an epoxy primer and a polyurethane topcoat, with phenolic microspheres, ground-up walnut shells, or washed and graded sand as a nonskid additive. The nonskid compound may be mixed with the epoxy paint, the polyurethane, or both, or sprinkled over the still-wet epoxy as described above. The paint is more expensive than an alkyd enamel, but the results should last as long as five years or more.

In our experience, success depends as much on surface preparation as on the type of paint used. A gelcoated fiberglass deck or a deck containing a waxed-resin surface laminate must be scrubbed with a solvent (acetone or a name-brand equivalent) to remove the wax, then sanded. As always, wear rubber gloves when working with solvents, and ensure ample ventilation.

Fiberglass Roving Non-Skid

Many workboats obtain a nonskid surface by laminating down heavy fiberglass cloth or roving over a wooden deck and simply painting over this rough surface. The aesthetics of this approach are debatable, since it imparts a very unfinished look (reminiscent of burlap) to the deck, but there's little doubt that it provides a good grip. It may also be painted with any of the available nonskid deck paints. Workboat operators use old barn paint or deck paint — anything they have on hand.

Chapter Eleven
Fiberglass Gelcoat

Options

Even with the best of regular care, the time will come when you look at your vintage fiberglass hull lying alongside a fresh, out-of-the-mold glass boat and decide it's time to spruce her up.

The easiest way to paint fiberglass is to take your boat to the best yard around, specify the finest two-part polyurethane paint and hand them a signed check. For most of us, though, repainting means doing it ourselves, and there's no reason why a reasonably competent owner shouldn't be able to do a quality job. Once you've decided to paint the boat yourself, the first step is to choose the type of paint. The two questions you should ask yourself are how skilled am I with paint and how much money do I wish to spend?

The two basic choices are a two-part polyurethane in a brushable formulation — unless you're a whiz with a spray gun and equipped to spray the professional mix, or an alkyd marine paint. The alkyd will require fewer coats because it can be applied slightly thicker for better coverage. The alkyd is less a thoroughbred paint and therefore it's easier to use and less expensive. On the other hand, it won't last as long as a two-part polyurethane, won't retain color quite as well, and won't have the surface abrasion resistance. Alkyds usually use mineral spirits as the solvent system, though some im-proved ones use silicone and acrylic resins to improve gloss retention and abrasion resistance. Alkyds are certainly the simplest system and as such are probably the best for first-time painters.

Gelcoating

The construction of a production boat in a female mold begins with a layer of gelcoat sprayed inside the waxed mold. A matrix of fiberglass, saturated with polyester resin, follows. The gelcoat is a protective surface layer of hard polyester resin that contains a pigment for appearance and resistance to sunlight. It also resists abrasion and protects the laminate from absorbing water. A breach in the gelcoat, such as a deep scratch or dimple that cracks the surrounding area, will allow water to enter the layup and eventually delaminate the matrix. Undamaged gelcoat is not 100 percent waterproof and will allow the hull to absorb water if it isn't periodically cleaned and waxed. One way to evaluate gelcoat porosity is to do a test patch with thinned paint. If there is more than usual porosity, tiny bubbles and depressions will appear over a period of a few minutes.

Gelcoat will absorb water and stains into its porous surface. Instead of scrubbing away at stubborn gelcoat stains with an abrasive cleaner or compound or wearing through it with sandpaper, first try a bleaching agent or detergent. Particularly for a new fiberglass hull, using an abrasive cleaner can be a mistake. An abrasive will scratch the surface, degrade the coating, and eventually give a better foothold for stains. A detergent solution applied with a sponge or soft cloth is a better bet for new hulls, at least for a first try, and stubbon spots can be treated again and again if the solution is working. Lemon juice is sometimes effective in removing stains that other solutions won't touch. Some toilet-bowl cleaners have a potent hydrochloric acid bleaching agent that sometimes works on stubborn stains. Clean the surface beforehand, then apply some of the bleaching agent with a soft, clean cotton cloth. Wear rubber gloves, rinse right away (at least until you get the feel of the bleach), and reapply in the worst areas. Keep rinsing vigorously. You may be able to use this treatment on boottop colors if they're hard and durable paint, and well seasoned, but it's always wise to do a test patch first.

In some cases gelcoat becomes deeply stained, and the only way to remove the discoloration is to remove the gelcoat. At this point you may have to decide whether to live with the stain or take off the gelcoating and paint over.

The last time I walked through our favorite marine store, I counted more than a dozen brands of fiberglass restoring and cleaning compounds. As with other marine finish products such as topside and bottom paints, certain types are favored in specific areas of the country, and sometimes they do work much better than others for local problems. Just as often, one dominant brand is the result of an enthusiastic distributor.

Fiberglass polishing compound is a very fine grit rubbing compound. Make sure you use a polishing compound and not a rougher grade rubbing compound, since the latter will abrade right through the thin gelcoat in a short time. Unless you have a large area to clean, you'd be wise to use hand pressure only and to rub back and forth in one direction instead of in a circular motion. A circular motion may produce swirl marks that will show up on the hull in certain light conditions. Careful use of a fine polishing compound can bring old, faded gelcoating to life by removing the surface layer, which can then be protected by waxing. Just don't rub too hard or too long in one place and be careful with power tools. Use low-rpm polishing tools.

Preparing Gelcoat For Painting

After a solvent wash, then a thorough soapy scrubbing and rinse, sand the entire hull with 220-grit paper, paying particular attention to repaired or rough spots that may need extra sanding with a rougher grit. You are preparing the hull for a primer coating so look carefully over the hull for shiny unsanded spots. This is when you should carefully inspect the entire hull to plan your next steps. Look out for the presence of mold-release waxes used in production. These waxes are sometimes tenacious and while they may clean easily in one area, they may be difficult to remove from other areas. Use your bare hand, as well as your eye, when inspecting the hull since your hand can often pick up slight differences in texture and fairness that

Rub gelcoated surfaces back and forth only, since a circular motion may leave swirls, especially on dark colors.

are barely visible to the eye. Unusually sticky or slick areas may indicate the presence of oil or wax, and if not removed with a solvent wash, then sanding, this contamination will foul all the following coatings that are applied.

Sanding gelcoat can be a tough job. Grits as coarse as 80 can be used for initial removal of surface material, as long as the surface is subsequently smoothed with finer grits and the sanding surface is applied thickly enough to cover the sanding scratches. Repair of damaged or weathered areas will obviously require the use of various more aggressive grits of paper. The usual choice for final sanding of the undercoating is 120, or perhaps 150 for two-part polyurethanes when you're striving for the finest finish possible.

Fill and sand any gouges, cracks, blisters, or other defects that will detract from a perfect finish. Since the undercoating will cover only the smallest defects, you should fill each imperfection and sand smooth before applying it. For filling surface scratches and nicks, you may choose from a number of products, but most finishers agree that two-part epoxy fillers are the most durable and give the best long-term results.

Surface dings in a fiberglass hull are often more easily detected after an initial sanding, especially if it was done using a block. Sanding takes off the surface sheen, making certain types of defects more visible.

Fill and sand any and all blemishes.

The primer coat is important because it provides the bond between the sanded hull and the new coating. A proper match of compatible undercoatings and paints is vital. We prefer to apply undercoating with a roller because it seems to lay down a more even and slightly thicker coating, and it helps the painting go more quickly. A good stiff brush will also work well. If, after light sanding with 150-grit paper, the hull still needs another coating of primer, apply as before and sand carefully. It adds considerable work to the job, but the results will pay off. Some painters recommend two coats of primer regardless of the condition of the hull. Always refer to the recommendations of the paint manufacturer to make sure you are using the correct primer. Some two-part paints may require a special undercoating or intermediate coating for best bonding. (Refer to Chapter 7, "Two-part Polyurethanes.")

If possible, get the hull indoors, in a large ventilated building, or at least under cover that will provide protection from sun, rain, and the evening dew. Two-part paints use some potent solvents, so good ventilation is a must when using these strong chemicals. Get some fans and arrange your ventilation. A fan placed right against a window to exhaust fumes promotes good air flow. The combination of an exhaust fan placed up high in the building and an intake fan on the opposite side of the building, down low, seems to work best. The paint job, whether two-part or alkyd, will benefit from comfortable working arrangements, as will your health. Successful paint jobs may be done outside with no cover at all, but much depends on the weather.

Gelcoat Repair

Most marine supply stores sell small repair tubes of gelcoat, with catalyst. If you can also obtain color pigment to match your hull, you're in business. Matching a faded or unusual color may be the hardest part of the job, and this is another reason to keep the repair area as small as possible. You can

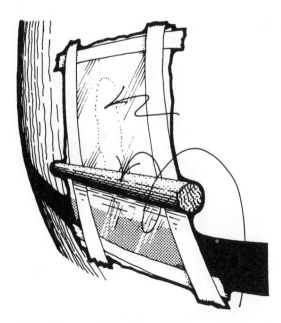

After the crack has been filled, sanded, and gelcoated, seal out air with a sheet of cellophane, and roll smooth with a dowel.

have your sample professionally matched, but it may be too expensive for a small repair. If you're trying to match the color on a broad topside, you might want to do a test sample in an obscure spot to see how the gelcoat looks when it cures, because it may change somewhat.

Gelcoat must be sealed from air in order to harden properly. After applying the catalyzed gelcoat onto the repair area, you must somehow seal the surface. PVA (polyvinyl alcohol), used for this purpose, is obtainable from boatyards that work in fiberglass. An easier method, especially for small repairs, is to use a piece of cellophane, wax paper, or transparent sandwich wrapping. With transparent wrapping you can visually inspect to ensure that no air bubbles are trapped underneath. Another advantage is that after the repair area is sealed, masked on the edges and airtight, you can roll over the repair with a wooden dowel or smooth it with a plastic squeegee. After the gelcoat kicks, remove the plastic wrap and sand carefully. Don't scratch up any more of the surrounding hull than necessary because all

these sanding marks will have to be removed with 400- and finally 600-grit paper. If you sand it too thin, go back and apply another coating.

Airbrushes are sometimes used to apply and feather gelcoat, but this is generally by experienced professionals equipped with all the necessary gear. A professional airbrush setup requires both a compressor and a practiced technique, but you can also get hobby-type airbrushes with aerosol cans of compressed air for propellant. One can of air is usually more than enough to do a number of small gelcoat repairs. Airbrushing allows excellent feathering action. Craze marks, for example, spread over a large area, are difficult to repair if they're too small to treat individually. This usually means spraying, and the aerosol-can airbrushes are often the least expensive solution. Hairline cracks must be filled by a squeegee or putty knife before spraying, and matching the color will still be the biggest problem.

Some boatyards repair gelcoat scratches with the types of filler commonly used in car body shops. These are polyester resin-based (this is the same basic polyester as in most fiberglass hulls), but when used in large amounts may in time shrink or crack. When filling large volume holes, it's better to use a fiberglass cloth and polyester resin mix, wetting out the fabric for the extra support and strength it gives, and painting over the repair. For larger structural repairs, epoxy is recommended.

Instead of spraying, you can also paint catalyzed gelcoating over the sanded and feathered filler, using a polyfoam brush or cheap bristle brush. Have three or four extra brushes on hand, because the resin and catalyst may disintegrate the brush. Throw the brush away if this starts to happen and grab another — if you wait too long, you'll end up with globs of foam in the gelcoating.

Epoxy Gelcoat Repair

Our preferred method, one that has never disappointed us in the long term, is to use

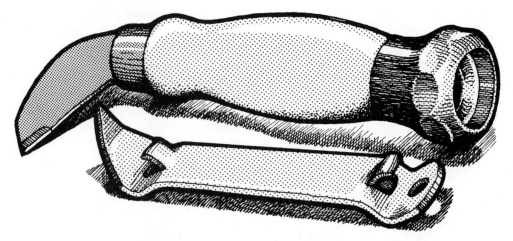

A can opener or Formica cutter are good for cleaning out scratches in preparation for gelcoat repair.

epoxy resin for repair and then paint over it with two-part polyurethane paint.

In order to isolate the repair area and to keep the rest of the topsides clean, we mask the work area and use heavy plastic around the scratch. Make sure the scratch is dry and clean. If there's any doubt, clean it with a sharp knife, a Formica cutting tool, or a sharp can opener. Sometimes a tiny scratch is easier to repair when gouged out slightly to provide a better bond for the repair resin. The most difficult scratches to repair are the ones that barely cut the surface.

After the scratch is isolated, cleaned, and dried, using heat lamps and fans if necessary to ensure absolute drying, coat the scratch with catalyzed epoxy resin and allow it to cure. One of the secrets of gelcoat repair is to

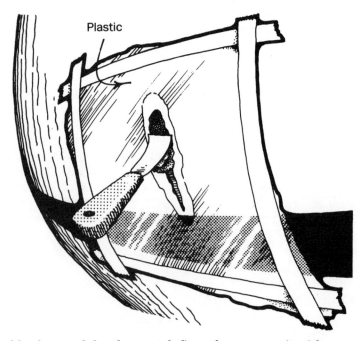

Thoroughly clean and dry the scratch first, then pre-wet it with epoxy and fill with a thickened mixture of epoxy and microballoons, stiff enough not to sag.

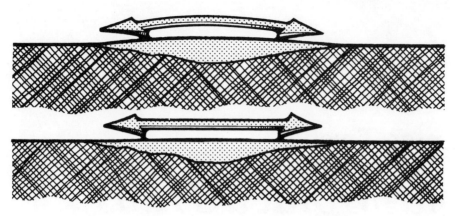

Let filling compound bulge slightly so that when it dries and shrinks it will be flush. This is especially important if using polyester filler.

keep the repair as small as the damage, or in other words, as small as possible. Then fill any depression in the surface, whether it be a tiny scratch or a deep gouge, with a thickened mixture of catalyzed epoxy resin and microballoons. Apply this mixture with a clean sharp putty knife. If it's a large hole, it's best to let it bulge up somewhat to ensure that it will later sand down flush with the surface. One good thing about an epoxy resin and microballoon mix is that it will not shrink like polyester resin fillers. We have seen large polyester patches that a month after repair have shrunk slightly below the surface of the hull. If you're working over-

head or for large repairs on a vertical surface, you add colloidal silica to stiffen the mix and prevent it from drooping. For ragged puncture holes in the hull, after the laminate is dried it should be swabbed with unthickened catalyzed epoxy to seal and provide the best bond for a thickened epoxy mixture. If the patch is difficult to level properly with a putty knife, a wide plastic squeegee may work best for applying the mix. The squeegee forces the epoxy deep into the hole and also leaves a good surface for sanding later. When the epoxy cures, sand with 360- or 400-grit paper and apply polyurethane paint to match.

Chapter Twelve
Cold-Molded Hulls

The cold-molded wood-epoxy matrix is a superb construction material, pound for pound among the stiffest boatbuilding materials available. There is little sense in building a cold-molded wooden boat with anything but epoxy for bonding, fiberglass sheathing, and final finish. Thus, what we are actually finishing is an epoxy-sealed surface, a stable, effective moisture barrier that offers an excellent seal for any type of coating.

The only real Achilles' heel of this system is that epoxy resin, like polyester, must be protected from the harmful long-term effects of sunlight. Since a boat's hull is bombarded with sunlight from above and from reflection off the water, protective paint or a good sunscreen is doubly important.

Sanding The Cold-Molded Hull

Most cold-molded hulls have an exterior layer of veneer or heavier planking that runs diagonally to the lamination it covers. (Wood as thick as ⅛ inch is usually considered veneer.) Some molded hulls have final fore-and-aft laminations, which make for a planked look while retaining the advantages of wood-epoxy construction. However these final laminations are arranged, they must be carefully sanded to remove fairing marks, especially if the hull is to be finished bright. Final fairing of cold-molded hulls is

done with floats and much cross sanding, and the process will usually leave a number of sandpaper tracks in the wood. If the hull is to be painted, the process is simplified because the undercoating hides these sanding marks. On boats finished bright, it will be necessary to do a final, careful sanding strictly with the grain.

Red cedar is particularly vulnerable to the marks left by cross sanding. A light and attractive wood for cold-molding, it is soft and will easily scratch and bruise. In fact, any species of cedar may take a bruise or scratch during the building and fairing process that only shows up after the first coating of epoxy is applied. Spruce is also soft and must be handled with care to prevent bruise marks that may become apparent when you wet out the wood with that first coat of epoxy.

After fairing a hull with 60-grit, we normally sand red cedar with a sanding block and by hand, moving only with the grain, with 80- and 100-grit. The important thing is to remove sanding marks, regardless of whether the hull is to be sheathed with fiberglass cloth or just sealed with epoxy, and 100-grit is amply fine to accomplish this.

If the cold-molded hull has just been sheathed, you may need to squeegee or roll additional coatings of epoxy into the fabric to fill the weave for a mirror-smooth surface, and very light sandings, or scrapings with a sharp furniture scraper, or both, are

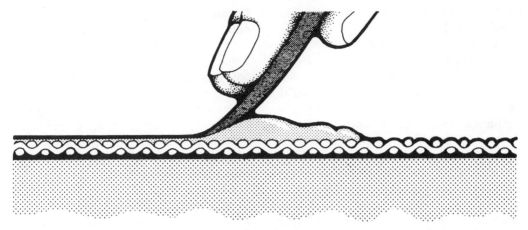

Fill the weave with a squeegee after the first saturation coat of epoxy has already kicked.

helpful. A scraper pulled lightly across the surface will immediately show any surface imperfections and does not produce fine dust as does sanding. A sharp scraper also cuts a very fine, controlled shaving, which will level a high spot. Any joints or overlaps of cloth will also need additional sanding to bring them flush and smooth.

If the sheathing cloth is light, 4 ounces or less, the wood strakes will show through quite well and the sheathing will be almost invisible. Heavier sheathings will develop more opacity. The hull will look good from a short distance away, but up close the weave of the glass fabric will usually be visible in places, although the effect is not unpleasant and will fade with time and exposure to sunlight.

Final Coating

The choice to be made at some step in construction, usually beforehand, is whether to finish bright or to paint the hull. Many cold-molded wood boats are designed to be finished bright to show off the wood strakes. Some are painted right away, and some are painted after a period of use or after some damage to the hull that almost necessitates a painted finish. If the decision is to finish bright, there are two popular choices available: multiple coatings of spar varnish with a good sunscreen, or multiple coatings of a clear two-part polyurethane paint. The characteristics, advantages, and disadvantages are discussed in the chapter on Brightwork.

Preparing a cold-molded epoxy-sealed hull for varnish or clear two-part polyurethane paint is similar to the same steps for painting a fiberglass hull except that no primer coat is needed. Wash the hull with a solvent to remove any trace of the waxy film that rises to the surface of a cured epoxy coating. Soap and water, or warm water and ammonia, followed by a light sanding will also remove this substance. Sand with 120- to 150-grit before applying the first coat of varnish or clear paint.

Cold-Molded Repair Technique

Effective and long-lasting repairs using epoxy and wood are not difficult, the only problem being to make an aesthetically acceptable repair on a bright wood hull. Surface gouges in a bright finished hull can be filled with a mixture of epoxy and microballoons, perhaps using some fine sanding dust from the same wood species for a better color match. This treatment is visible only with small localized damage, and even very small scratches filled this way may be visible on a bright hull.

If a cold-molded hull has small white or opaque impact spots with crushed wood fibers and damaged fiberglass, it may be necessary to cut out those areas and refill them. Small, isolated areas of impact can sometimes be sanded well and saturated with multiple coatings of epoxy until the surface is flush, but major areas of damage may require glass cloth laid into the depression created by removing the old glass. Such repairs also become structural. Sand a smooth 1-inch to 2-inch feathered edge around the perimeter of the spot damage, lay in the glass cloth, and saturate with epoxy. Come back later to fill and sand any edges or low spots with epoxy.

For larger, more serious damage, you have numerous options to make an effective repair. Planing off a layer of damaged veneer and replacing with new veneer is a good technique. For hull punctures, complete repair will often require large and flexible butt blocks fastened inside the hull and used as a foundation for building up layers of veneer. The ends of each subsequent layer should be butted to the existing veneer a bit farther beyond the perimeter of the puncture, until the repair is built out flush to the hull surface. The last layer should be careful-

ly fitted to match the surrounding veneer in color and grain direction. There is usually a very apparent difference of color between older exposed wood and new veneer, but this will dissipate somewhat in time. The most challenging part of such repairs is fitting the ends of the new veneer to the existing pieces. For a painted hull this is not a problem, but a clear-finished hull requires some care in fitting and will probably never look as good as the original.

A butt joint is about the best solution to hiding the ends of a veneer repair, since a scarph joint may show more conspicuously at its feathered edge. If the gouge is near the waterline and the veneer runs diagonally, you might be able to extend one end of the repair beneath the waterline and leave only one butt joint visible. Alternately, you might be able to run a piece of veneer all the way to the rub rail and hide it that way. As veneer ages it mellows somewhat, and a repair will become less apparent as exposure time lengthens. Don't stain the repair, because that would weaken the epoxy bond.

Digging out a single layer of veneer is not as difficult as it seems. You can use the epoxy glue line as an indicator of proper depth. It might further simplify the job to run around the perimeter of the repair area with a router and sharp carbide cutter bitt.

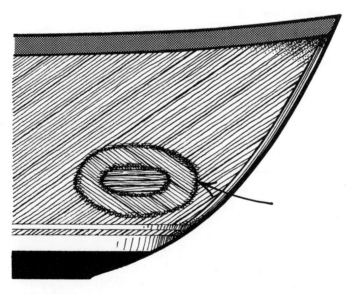

Glue lines can be used as a guide for planing off damage.

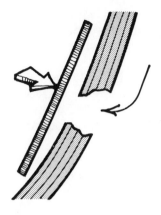
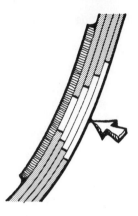

Complete repair of hull punctures may require butt blocks as a foundation for the building up of carefully fitted veneers.

Set the bitt to just less than ⅛ inch for veneer, or however deep you wish to cut, and rout around and across the area you have to remove. If you criss-cross the repair area with the router, you will be able to use these score marks as a guide in removing veneer. This process will also provide an opportunity to see how efficiently epoxy works as a glue and laminating adhesive.

Finishing Plywood

Plywood is an excellent boatbuilding material that combines dimensional stability and strength with light weight. Before veneers became readily available, many cold-molded boats were built from plywood door skins of ⅛-inch thickness. For larger hulls, we have used ¼-inch and sometimes ⅜-inch plywood strips in double and triple laminations, all bonded and sealed with epoxy. Quality plywood is also about the best available material for bulkheads in any type of hull because it adds so much strength to the structure and provides the natural look of wood with light weight. A plywood bulkhead can be very attractive in a fiberglass or aluminum hull.

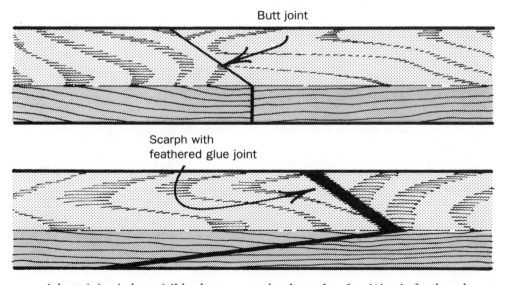

A butt joint is less visible than a scarph where the glue joint is feathered.

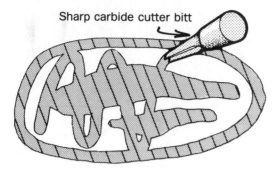

Sharp carbide cutter bitt

Set bitt to desired depth and rout around damaged area, crisscrossing for depth guide.

Most plywood is constructed from opposing laminations of rotary-cut veneer held together with waterproof glue. Domestic marine plywood commonly uses the same glue as exterior grades of plywood. The difference in marine, or AA, grade is usually the number and quality of the laminations and the absence of voids. In order for the sheet of ply to bend uniformly and resist forces evenly, all the laminations should be nearly equal in thickness, and if possible the sheet should have an even number of laminations so that an equal number are oriented in each direction. The weak point of a plywood panel is the end of the sheet, which has little resistance to water absorption and must therefore be well sealed to ensure longevity and full strength. When using epoxy, such as in a cold-molded construction, the edges are normally encapsulated in large fillets on both sides to ensure watertightness and a reliable bond to the hull sides. Without benefit of epoxy it may take some extra effort to seal the plywood edges. Fungicidal bedding compound helps prevent rot but sometimes does little to seal an edge from water. Three or more coats of paint or saturating oil are also effective if you apply them with patience and care.

Sometimes the face of a sheet of softwood plywood will present unique finishing problems. The veneers of plywood are peeled from a log, like pulling paper towels from the roll, and the annual softwood growth rings come off in strips. This presents a varying surface of hard, resinous wood alternating with softer, sometimes spongy bands of wood; as a result it takes paint unevenly. Sanding to level the surface sometimes digs out the softer wood even more, leaving the hardwood standing proud. One method for leveling the face of the sheet is to use a sharp, wide, and relatively long hand plane. Another option, when painting, is to sand lightly and leave it alone, letting the wood pattern show through the finish.

Bare plywood, like all bare wood, needs a good sealer in the form of a prime coat or even a special plywood sealer, available from some plywood manufacturers. Sometimes a thinned topcoat is used for a sealer. Even plywood used in boat interiors usually needs at least three coatings — a seal or prime coat and two topcoats, which are usually enamel for interior finish. Most hardwood plywood, such as imported lauan and higher-quality types, will take paint and epoxy more evenly than domestic softwood plywood because growth rings are much less distinguishable.

Although most plywood takes epoxy well, domestic fir-faced plywood is an exception. Fir plywood needs to be sheathed with fiberglass cloth in order to prevent hairline cracks from developing on the surface. Once sheathed with even the lightest cloth, the problem is completely eliminated.

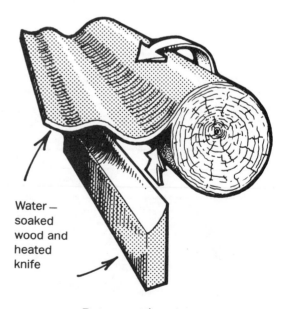

Water — soaked wood and heated knife

Rotary cutting veneer.

When using epoxy on plywood for important structural members, there is a little trick you can use to locate any holes or voids in the laminations. A void in the interior laminations, running almost full length in the plywood, could be a waterway to soak an entire sheet. After epoxy is applied and has cured for a day or so, run your bare hand over the surface and listen; any voids inside the plywood will produce a slightly altered tone. With practice you will be able to locate even the smallest of voids in the lamination. If voids are present in a critical location in the structure, it may be worthwhile to dig them out and fill them with a thickened epoxy mix.

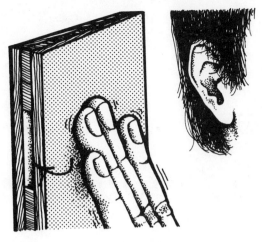

"Listening" for voids in the plywood.

Chapter Thirteen

Boottops and Sheer Stripes

Hull graphics have come a long way. A few years ago, about all you saw in a marina was plain white on white hulls, single boottops, and perhaps a thin cove stripe here and there. Along with a fair and pleasing sheer line, a clean, straight boottop does a lot to finish off and complement a hull. In addition to the boot above the bottom paint, some boats with broad topsides make particularly good use of bold sheer stripes and other colorful graphics to lower the visual profile and provide a streamlined look to an otherwise boxy hull.

A well-done boottop or sheer stripe is a pleasure to look at, but an unfair boottop or stripe is worse than none at all. Mistakes, particularly those near the waterline, are readily apparent to anyone with a good eye.

Finding the Waterline

Some boats come from the builder with the designer's boottop and boot bottom scribed on the hull. This is the design waterline (DWL) at which the boat should float for predicted design performance. The usual and more realistic practice, however, especially for cruising boats, is to keep raising the waterline and boot as the load displacement increases. It's a regular ritual for cruising boats as the gear keeps accumulating.

Some boat owners, if they are unsure of the waterline or are dealing with an irregular shape such as a hard-chine hull, might be better off to launch the boat, load it, haul it after a week or so, and use the scum line as a reference for the bottom paint and boottop. It will certainly give a truthful line for trim and actual displacement of the hull.

Leveling The Hull

Before you mark a waterline for painting or scribing, it's necessary first of all to have the hull dead level. This is best done by the builder while the hull is still on the building base, at which time the designer's calculations are used to obtain reference points for the boottop. When you mark a waterline on an older boat you will probably have to resort to the plan's drawings to ensure that you are working from the correct reference points. Without plans drawings, the scum line is still one of the best and most honest reference points. Keep in mind that if you plan to alter the trim by removing an engine, adding an engine, repositioning fuel tanks, etc., you will have to remark the waterline.

Faced with the task of leveling a hull that is out of the water, you will need to refer to obviously level structures designed into the boat, such as cabin soles, counter tops, engine bed stringers or other built-in items that are supposedly parallel with the waterline. If you find broad discrepancies, about the best you can do, short of launching to get a scum line, is to average the best references you can obtain and ignore those that dis-

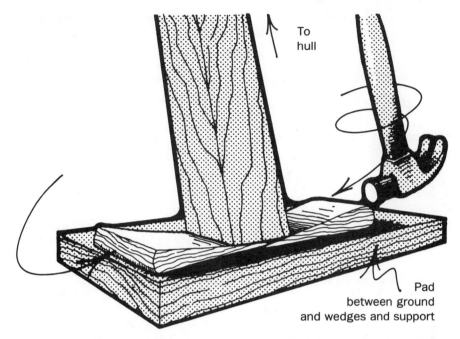

Adjusting the height of a support is very gradual and easy to control when using hardwood wedges.

agree. Once you have your reference points, it's just a matter or raising or lowering the hull a little at a time until you perfectly level the boat, fore and aft and side to side.

Wedges are very useful for leveling. Placed under appropriate supports, they raise the hull in small increments. Using long, narrow hardwood wedges, you can raise large, heavy hulls slowly and with complete control by tapping the wedges with a hammer. A hull must be well braced on both sides before you begin to lift. Uprights with diagonals for support are usually required. If the hull is in a cradle, the cradle itself can be leveled, but you need access to as much of the waterline area as possible and room to eyeball the lines.

The Water-Level Method

After the hull is level, and you have at least one trusted reference mark for the height of the bottom paint, you can use any number of methods to mark additional reference points around the hull. A transit is fine if you have one and you're familiar with its use; it must be moved at least once,

possibly more, to do both sides of the hull. The high-tech solution is a laser beam. More commonly used, especially for small boats, is the simple water level, which does a fine job. Following the principle that water seeks its own level, a transparent hose or a length of clear tubing is filled with water and led under and around to reach both sides of the hull. This is a two-person job, and it requires that one person stay on the "control" position while the other moves around the hull marking reference points.

Fill the hose almost full of water; you may need to carry a small jug around to top it off once you're in position. Get all the air bubbles out of the line by "walking" the hose, lifting it to force the bubbles up and out one end. Station the control person at the starting reference point, which may be the bottom of the transom in some sailboats, or some other designer's measurement.

If you have to duck under scaffolding and around supports while getting into position, pinch off the end of the hose, or hold your thumb over the top to prevent water from shooting out when you move. If it

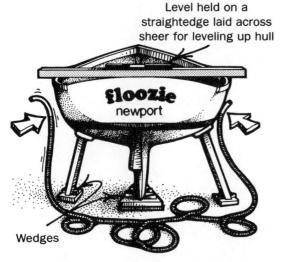

Level held on a straightedge laid across sheer for leveling up hull

Wedges

Water levels in a hose can be used to mark new waterlines.

spills, add more. Movement of the hose will cause the water to oscillate, so as the marker moves to a new location, he or she should place the hose against the side of the hull and hold it steady, while the control person moves the hose up or down until the water level at the control position end agrees with the reference point. When the control water level agrees with reference marks on the hull, the control person calls, ''mark,'' and the other person marks the water level on the hull.

On near-vertical surfaces, intervals of 6 to 12 inches between marks are usually sufficient to produce a fair line, but on more sloping surfaces, such as over a chine or sloping transom, it may be necessary to place marks much closer.

At this time you may mark the top and bottom of the boot. If you wish to add multiple stripes above the DWL, a mark can be placed for the top and bottom of each stripe. If you plan to use multiple stripes or a very wide stripe, it's a good idea to mark extra reference points with the water level, although as long as you have one continuous correct line on the hull, you can at a later time use a square and level to obtain lines above or below the reference line.

Multiple stripes are relatively easy to lay

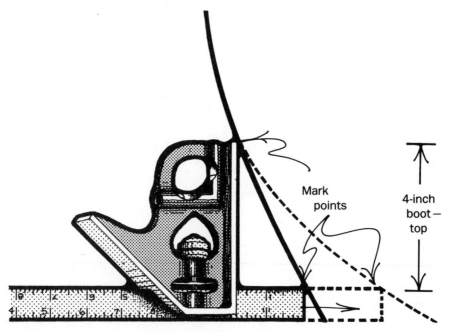

Mark points

4-inch boot— top

You can mark a boottop stripe on hull topsides using an adjustable square with a level and a sliding rule. As the shape of the hull changes from near vertical at bow to near horizontal at the transom, rule is extended until it meets the hull again.

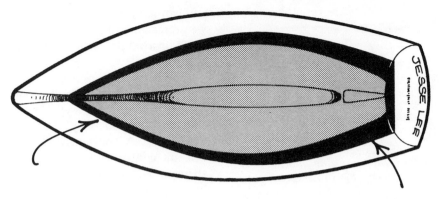

Boottop as seen from below, showing varying width as hull shape changes.

out and paint, as long as you understand that a waterline is not constant in width as it moves around a shaped hull. If the hull were shaped like a shoebox, with perfectly vertical sides, then boottops could be painted the exact same width all around the hull, but since this is seldom the case, all boottops vary in width as they move from near-vertical hull sides close to the bow to sloping areas around the transom.

A narrow space between the bottom paint and the stripe adds crispness and definition to a hull. It means slightly more work, but the effect is often worthwhile. Multiple boottops, often of contrasting colors, also cut down the visual profile of the hull. They look especially good on certain non-traditional hull types, such as ultra-lights and multihulls.

After reference marks are made all around the hull, sand and apply masking tape in preparation for painting. Pro-quality thin-line masking tape is more expensive, but it's by far the best if you're striving for a clean sharp line.

Use wide tape for stripe layout; it's easier to handle and seems to fair much better. Narrow tape twists and sometimes takes un-fair shapes when you apply it to a sloping hull. One person, the one with the better or more experienced eye, should judge the fair-ness of the stripe while the other applies the tape in sections to the hull. The tape can be pulled off easily and reapplied to correct "wows" in the stripe. Errors often do not become apparent until the tape is stuck to the hull, so it's important to work with small sections at a time, progressing around the

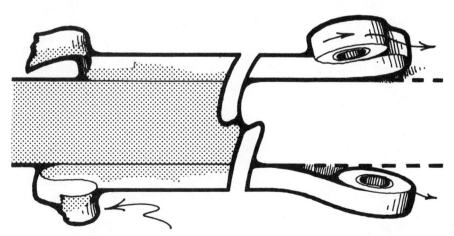

Align tape along marks and press edge down firmly for a clean line. Remove tape well before the paint sets.

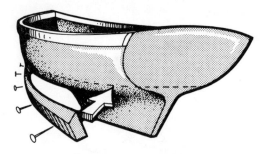

A batten placed on waterline marks may help in "eyeballing" the fairness of your new line.

hull and correcting as you go. Use high-quality tape, pushing the edge down hard once you're satisfied that the line is fair. Pull the tape soon after the paint is applied, or at least well before it sets, to prevent pulling up chips of dried paint with the tape.

Although masking tape works well, particularly in wider widths (which seem to highlight unfairness better than thin widths), an alternative for wooden hulls is to tack on a flexible wood batten instead of using masking tape. The batten should be as stiff as possible to maintain fairness, yet still flexible enough to bend around all sections of the hull. Very large hulls are usually the best candidates for this treatment because the wood batten will provide a line that some people find somewhat easier to judge than masking tape. As an example, for a 30-foot heavy-displacement double-ender, we used a pine batten ¼-inch thick and 2 inches wide. Tack the top edge even with the reference marks on the hull. You still have to remove the batten and apply masking tape before you paint.

If you plan to scribe or incise a line into the hull, usually a batten is necessary as a guide. The scribing may be done in sections by moving the batten around the hull, but each time the batten is moved it should be allowed plenty of overlap to extend the line accurately. If you have a lot of confidence,

you can use a router to cut hull grooves, but we prefer a hand implement such as a sharp knife or a single-tooth carbide Formica cutting tool.

There are also pressure-sensitive plastic waterline tapes, and the best quality stick and wear reasonably well. They sometimes chip or break but they are easier to apply than paint. A constant-width strip of tape will not conform to actual waterline width all around a hull, but it might be appropriate for defining or outlining a waterline. Before applying the tape, scrub the hull with a solvent such as acetone to remove wax, sand very lightly as necessary to remove a high gloss, wash with soap and water, and dry well. One person is still needed to apply the tape while another eyeballs for a fair line.

Sheer Stripes

Sheer stripes usually run parallel to the sweeping sheer of the hull. They may be wider forward than aft, have a constant width, or lie in any pleasing arrangement to suit the hull and rig. They may be continuous or interrupted. The best way to design a sheer stripe is to start with a large-scale profile drawing of the hull. Draw a pleasing shape and make your mistakes on the paper before you touch brush to hull. When you have drawn what looks to be the best, measure with a scale ruler the distances from the sheer down, the waterline up, or both. Apply reference marks and then tack on a batten or apply masking tape right to the hull and fair the tape. Eyeball it from all directions before you paint; what looks good from forward may look terrible from the side. You'll need to prepare the surface for paint by sanding and cleaning well. Two-part paints, with their superior performance, provide a long-lasting stripe that wears well and retains its original color longer than most other types. Two-part polyurethane paint is very good for bright, bold colors.

Chapter Fourteen

Bottom Paints

The best methods for protecting and maintaining the bottom of any particular boat depends on the area in which it's moored, the facilities available, and the temperature, salinity, or any special conditions of the water. Brackish water, strong tidal flows, currents, and pollution, among other factors, can affect what happens under the waterline. The best sources of specific local knowledge are other boat owners, shipyards, and professional yacht maintainers in that area. They have learned what works best through a process of trial and error, and usually can save the novice boat owner time, money, and frustration. Every area seems to have formulations that, for one reason or another, work better than others.

Types and Components

The traditional bottom treatment is copper paint. This is available in a variety of formulations, types, and strengths, and is often mixed with tin and other substances that are poisonous to grass, worms, barnacles, and algae. Sheet copper was once tacked onto ships' bottoms to protect them from worms and barnacles and is still used in some parts of the world, but anti-fouling paint is by far the easiest and least expensive approach.

Two basic components make up traditional bottom paints: the vehicle or binding agent, which includes coloring and solvents; and the anti-fouling agent, copper (cuprous oxide) and sometimes tin or a mixture of ingredients.

Boat owners now have a variety of types of coatings from which to choose, including traditional soft or hard copper bottom paints, tin-based paints, vinyl paints, epoxy paints, Teflon-based coatings, super-hard epoxy/graphite non-anti-fouling, and the new copolymer bottom paints that promise the best performance yet, but with increasing controversy about the health hazards involved in their use. Some ingredients, such as gunpowder and cayenne pepper that users

claim add potency to the bottom paint, have local appeal. Whether or not shipworms prefer spice with their meals is debatable. To further complicate the situation, certain years show an increase of marine growth, a peak in the cycle of algae bloom for example, and nothing but hauling and repainting will keep the bottom clean.

Hard Versus Soft Paint

Soft bottom paints are usually the choice for displacement hulls, which need an anti-fouling mixture that leaches poison steadily from its surface. Fast hulls that use speed to help keep the bottom clean most often can use hard bottom paint to advantage. Hard paints provide a smoother surface, causing less resistance to movement through the water. They improve performance and save fuel in motorboats, while in sailboats they increase sailing ability in both light airs and heavy. They also stick better than a soft paint.

Since hard bottom paints rely on speed to help keep the hull clean, it makes little sense to use it, even on a fast boat, if you plan to putter about or anchor for days at a time. A soft bottom paint would better protect the bottom.

Changing Bottom Paints

As boats move to different locations, and conditions and opinions change, a boat owner may wish to try another type of bottom paint. Beware of compatibility problems with some types — it pays to try a test patch on a small area if there is any doubt.

About the only thing that can be applied over soft copper paint is more soft copper paint. The general and logical rule is that soft coatings can be applied over hard coatings, but hard coatings cannot be applied over a soft coating. Hard finishes usually require just a sanding before recoating, but soft coatings may contain tiny pits or craters caused by uneven leaching and wearing, and usually require a scraping or hard sanding to provide a uniform surface for recoating.

Applying Traditional Bottom Paints

Mixing

It's important to mix bottom paint thoroughly, and to continue mixing the paint as it's applied to prevent solids from settling to the bottom of the can. Improper mixing can mean the paint goes on with inconsistent amounts of anti-fouling compound, and this may cause the hull to foul unevenly. The paint may also dry in different shades, which is a clue that it needed more mixing during application. The solution to unevenness is to apply another well-mixed coating.

When you open a new can of bottom paint, you probably won't be able to stir it vigorously without slopping paint all over, so it's best to pour about a third of the can

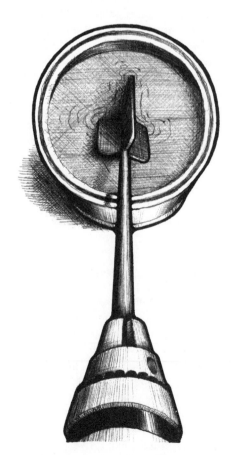

A paddle on an electric drill makes a good mixer.

into another clean container. Then stir with a clean, wide, flat-bottomed paddle. Scrape the bottom of the can to break up any solids that may have settled and mix until they are suspended in the paint. Some yards use a wide paddle on an electric drill. Stir with a lifting motion to bring the contents of the bottom up to the surface. As you complete the mixing slowly pour the smaller quantity of paint back into the original can, stirring as you do so. If the cans are almost equal in size, some painters like to pour the paint back and forth from can to can to ensure that all the solids are well mixed. This mixing technique is sometimes called "boxing."

Thinning

Use only the recommended thinner and as little of it as possible, just enough to make the paint spreadable. Most manufacturers discourage the excessive use of thinners, feeling it reduces the potency of the paint, but it's better to thin the paint so it applies easily, and apply more coatings, than to struggle along with ropey paint that refuses to flow and adhere properly to the bottom.

Flag Colors

When you apply bottom paint in layers, it may be helpful to use different colors for each coat. Apply extra coats along the waterline since water flow and wear is increased in this area. That way you can see at a glance if coverage is complete, especially when you're reaching down under a darkened bilge or keel. After the boat's been in the water for some time, and another color appears, you'll have a much more precise idea of wear and the thickness of paint left in that area. Some painters call these *flag* or *sign* colors.

Rollers and Brushes For Bottom Paint

Rollers are a good, fast means of applying bottom paint, and may be fitted with long handles to make it easier to reach under the bilge and keel. Bottom painting is difficult enough, especially overhead work, and handles of various lengths can make for an easier and much better job.

Sometimes rollers don't apply certain types of paint quite as smoothly as brushes, but a lot also depends on the type of surface, and the skill of the painter. A roller may even do a better job than a brush in the hands of a novice. Sometimes another painter can follow right behind a roller with a brush, smoothing ridges and ripples for a more uniform job, but since the solvents in many bottom paints "flash" away so quickly, the time during which the paint can be smoothed is often very short. The solvents evaporate into the atmosphere, and the paint becomes almost immediately tacky, especially in warm weather or in direct sunlight. Wind also speeds evaporation of solvents.

Rollers sometimes provide a clean pass on the upper hull side and dribble a ridge of paint onto the hull on the downhill side, but it's a simple matter to make rapid overlapping strokes to get a clean surface. When painting an older wood hull or a rough surface with a roller, it may be best to roll on the paint with vertical strokes and finish with a fore-and-aft stroke to smooth the paint. Stroking in more than one direction, assuming you have time, is usually the best way to apply a more uniform coating. Hard, racing paints are often applied to align with the direction of water flow across the hull.

If you're forced to work fast, it's better to strive for your best effort with roller alone and forget the brush, except for cutting in against the boottop. Or if you must, add thinner in very small amounts to give more working time.

You may want to experiment with various types of rollers and nap thickness for your chosen type of paint and technique. A heavier nap may work best with a thinner paint because it holds more and can be rolled over an area a second and third time to spread properly. A short nap will usually provide more even coverage for thicker paints that spread well, without needing to hold a lot of paint in the roller. Foam rollers are sometimes good for bottom paints as long as the solvents in the paint don't affect the foam. Polyfoam brushes can also sometimes be used effectively to apply paint in

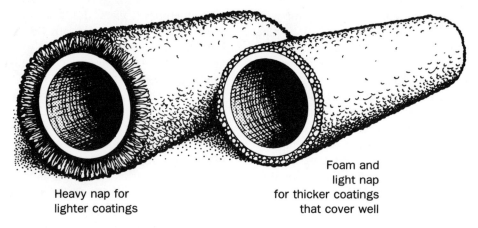

Heavy nap for
lighter coatings

Foam and
light nap
for thicker coatings
that cover well

You can vary the nap on your roller to suit the job.

crevices and for cutting in, and are usually thrown away at the end of the job. Here's where throwaway brushes can save money and time spent on cleanup.

Be careful about using old rollers that have not been cleaned properly. They may have solid encrustations that prevent them from holding the right amount of paint, or spreading and laying on the paint evenly. The same goes for brushes. Old brushes are perfectly all right for bottom painting if they're cleaned well and the bristle is straight and healthy. Old floppy brushes are not the best because you end up mopping the paint on instead of brushing. The side of the bristle doesn't hold enough paint, nor does it apply it evenly. Whether you're using a roller or brush, stop and resaturate often without allowing it to run completely dry. The object with bottom paint is to apply a uniform coating rather than just cover the surface.

Keep a supply of polyfoam brushes on hand.

Coating Thickness

With most bottom paint it's usually wise to lean toward a thick coating, rather than thin, because thickness often means more and longer-lasting protection. Don't try to make the paint go farther than it's designed to go, but don't try to slap it on in one too-thick coating. If you have paint left over, go back over the hull, applying an extra layer in vulnerable areas such as the keel bottom or the bow area and waterline on a faster boat. If there are bare, worn, and abraded spots where the bottom paint is gone, you may need to sand and prime these areas before applying bottom paint. A lack of proper primer coat may have been the reason for these bare spots in the first place, and such a coat will ensure a good bond this time.

Primer

In order for bottom paint to adhere well to bare wood bottoms, the wood should be seasoned as well as possible. Since it's rare in this country to build a hull with wet, unseasoned wood, this usually poses no problem. Green wood's high moisture content and resulting dimensional instability will often cause problems with paint of any kind.

Bare wood treated with oil and wood preservative, as it generally is in traditionally built wooden hulls, should cause no unusual problems with the initial bottom paint coats if the oil and wood preservative have been allowed at least 48 hours to saturate and dry.

If you have the option, check with the manufacturer of the bottom paint type you intend to use before you apply any wood preservative or other treatment.

For wood bottoms, whether not painted previously or later sanded and scraped down to bare wood, the first coats of bottom paint are usually thinned 10 percent for slightly improved penetration. This primer coat should be applied to all accessible underwater areas, including inside any open seams. Caulking is normally completed before bottom painting, but a builder may choose to caulk and fair the seams with a recommended seam compound after the prime coat. Much depends on whether the builder is using strictly traditional caulkings of oakum and cotton, or modern caulkings out of a cartridge. In either case, after the seams are filled and flush and the prime coat is on, the second coating of bottom paint is usually applied full-strength and the boat is launched after the recommended drying time.

Aluminum hulls require a special primer coat under the waterline, as does fiberglass, except that copper-based paint is not recommended for use on aluminum hulls because it tends to interact with aluminum to create galvanic action. Most manufacturers offer a special type of coating, with a more inert anti-fouling ingredient for use on aluminum.

When you prepare a new fiberglass hull for the first coat of bottom paint, wash it thoroughly with solvent to remove any trace of mold release wax. Use cheese cloth or other rough absorbent cloth for scrubbing to help remove the wax from stubborn spots. Turn or fold the cloth often as you scrub. Most manufacturers have a recommended fiberglass primer, which is applied by brush or roller and allowed to cure, after which the bottom should not be handled or sanded. The bottom paint is applied full-strength or thinned only as necessary for application. Apply the recommended number of coatings.

Cleaning

A smooth surface not only is easier to scrub clean of slime, but helps deter bottom

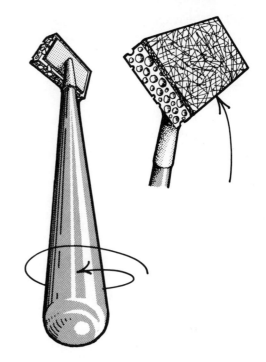

A sponge faced with a tough scrubber and attached to a long handle makes bottom cleaning easier.

growth. Tiny ripples, bumps, or defects in the coating give algae and other creatures a better foothold.

A light rubdown while the bottom is still wet will often revive exhausted bottom paint by removing slime and surface accumulation that may be blocking the proper release of toxins. Use a folded rag, a high-pressure hose, or a sponge with a scouring pad on the back. If the bottom needs more-aggressive, abrasive action for cleaning, use a stiff brush, scraper, or burlap bags filled with sand.

Hard bottom paints tend to build up in thick coatings more easily than soft paints, which continually leach themselves off the hull. Hard vinyl paints may begin to chip after a number of coatings have been applied. When this happens you should probably remove the paint and start with a new base coat. Vinyl-based paints are the hardest to remove and usually require rough, hard sanding. Chemical paint removers seldom work well on bottom paints.

Complete Coverage

Take the time to move blocks and slings to alternate locations during the paint job in order to get complete coverage. Use wedges, levers, and braces to support the hull while you move blocks around and paint. Instead of chasing behind the Travelift or crane, trying to dab paint on those bare spots as the boat lowers into the water — try to do it while you're finishing the rest of the hull. The bottom of the keel may be hard to paint with a brush, so you might use a roller with a short or long handle. If the keel's almost on the ground, a mirror will help you to check for good coverage.

Safety Considerations

Bottom paint is by design toxic and therefore potentially dangerous to humans. Even the mildest formulations will cause problems for some people, and susceptibility may vary from person to person. Having once spent a week in mild but constant pain wearing a dark eye patch from a tiny flake of old bottom paint that flipped into my eye, I can attest to the danger of the stuff. Working overhead is particularly risky, whether removing old paint or applying new. A roller will sometimes flip drops, and brushes will spatter when the bristles extend. Wear a long-brimmed cap when you work overhead, and tight goggles when you work over or underneath a hull. A good, tight respirator is necessary when you sand, and good ventilation helps dissipate solvent fumes.

Epoxy/Graphite Bottom Treatment

The ultimate in hard bottom finishes for performance hulls may be epoxy/graphite. This is most often used on racing boats and other small craft that are hauled regularly for maintenance, scrubbing, or storing because epoxy/graphite has *no* anti-fouling capability. It can, however, be polished to a very slick surface that may be waxed to make it even smoother. The low-friction surface can be rubbed clean of slime when the boat is hauled.

Epoxy/graphite works best on fiberglass hulls that are properly prepared for the

A good, tight respirator is necessary when you sand.

epoxy coating, or on cold-molded or ply-wood hulls that are sheathed with fiberglass. For traditional plank-on-frame wood boats, this is a risky treatment at best, and usually won't last long enough to make it practical, since the planks will absorb water and swell too much to provide a good base for the epoxy. Used on wet, rotted, previously oiled, or older unsheathed plywood, it may eventually crack and flake away, allowing water to have even easier access.

Epoxy/graphite is very durable and abrasion-resistant; in fact, it's almost impossible to sand. It has been used successfully on everything from racing hulls to our white-water dories that run through the Grand Canyon. It also lends structural stiffening to the hull. It works best on tight hulls that provide a stable, dry base and it is our choice of bottom treatment for lightweight rowing and fishing dories.

Epoxy/Graphite Mixing and Application

Sand the hull smooth with 80- or 100-grit paper. Fill and fair any dings in the hull with an epoxy-based filler. Use with small batches of catalyzed epoxy to control heat buildup in the resin and work in the shade if possible. (The graphite powder will blacken the epoxy resin, which will absorb sunlight and accelerate heat buildup, particularly on hot days.)

Mix graphite powder with catalyzed epoxy at about 20 to 25 percent by volume. Stir well and apply with a foam roller. For small hulls, you may wish to cut a roller to a smaller size for better control on rounded hull surfaces. Roll on the mixture as smoothly as possible and follow with a brush, if necessary, to take out bubbles. We apply three to five coatings, allowing each to kick before the next coating, and scrape or sand lightly if necessary to remove imperfections in the surface. With reasonable care, you can obtain a mirror finish on a hull with this method, which will add considerable abrasion protection at the same time. Used on the bottom of an ultra-light dory, it provides noticeable stiffness to its thin bottom and sides.

Copolymer Bottom Paints

Traditionally, bottom painting has been an annual ritual, whether a boat is kept in the water all year or hauled for the winter. Without an annual bottom job most boats develop a healthy salad garden under the waterline, a fuel-wasting layer of growth that also ruins performance under sail. A new type of bottom paint has been made available over the last few years. Developed originally for naval vessels, it can extend dramatically the effective life of a bottom job.

The new copolymer paints are chemically bonded and thus do not separate like traditional bottom paints, in which the toxins are suspended only by vigorous mixing. Traditional bottom paints dissipate their toxins into the water, leaving tiny craters and pits on the surface. Copolymers, by contrast, wear away in micro layers, much like a bar of soap, and remain effective as long as there is paint on the bottom. Copolymer paint will last in direct relation to the thickness of the coating and the number of coats applied; the thicker it is, the longer it will last. Copolymer bottom paints also retain their effectiveness in or out of the water.

The copolymers are probably as good or better than most hard vinyls or racing paints at producing a hard, friction-free surface and they may also be buffed to make them smoother. Copolymer's continuous "wash" provides a smoother surface, which cuts drag and makes eventual repainting much easier because preparation time and effort is much reduced.

Underwater rubdowns of copolymer paints will remove the accumulation of slime that, left on the hull, may retard the normal effective action of the paint. Like two-part polyurethane paints, copolymers were first designed for professional application only, but manufacturers quickly realized the benefits of making these bottom paints available to boat owners who want to do their own work. A few brands are now available to be rolled or brushed by the boat owner.

The effective life of a copolymer bottom paint job is difficult to predict accurately, but without unusual conditions and with a proper application, a boat owner can expect perhaps four years or maybe more. If zincs and other underwater hardware can be maintained without hauling, then you may save the time and bother of hauling for a number of years.

Copolymer bottom paints are applied like traditional types, and may also be applied in contrasting colors to help identify wear characteristics.

It should be emphasized that copolymer bottom paints are extremely toxic. They are restricted in some 17 states for that reason, and the Federal government may issue its own guidelines in 1987. Be scrupulous in utilizing safety gear such as proper gloves, full body coveralls, hat, goggles, and organic vapor masks, and in following the other precautions outlined at the beginning of this book.

Chapter Fifteen

Fiberglass Bottom Blistering

Blistering under the waterline has been a minor — and sometimes major — problem with fiberglass boats since the first one was built. In earlier decades, however, it did not appear to occur with the regularity seen nowadays. Until recent times we seldom saw the blistering problem spread over entire bottoms; rather, it was usually isolated bubbles here and there on the bottom. Some sources estimate that over half of today's fiberglass boats have this dermatological problem, while others say as little as 10 percent of glass hulls are affected; the correct answer probably lies somewhere between the two figures. From our personal experience we feel that only a small percentage are severely affected, but that a large percentage, perhaps even more than half, are slightly or intermittently affected. In the past, builders and manufacturers of materials may have passed the buck, but now that the problem is apparent, all involved are making sincere efforts to solve it.

The Problem

What exactly is the problem? Small bubbles appear under the waterline, not just under the bottom paint but under the gelcoat. The gelcoat is there to protect the polyester/fiberglass matrix, the laminate that forms the hull. When water gets under the gelcoat, it also soaks into the resin and fiberglass cloth, weakening and delaminating the matrix. If you've ever seen a boat with a large area of water-soaked fiberglass below the waterline you know what a mess wet fiberglass can be.

The blisters aren't always tiny, nickel-and-dime-sized things. Left unchecked they can increase in size and eventually, in extreme cases, could soak their way right through a hull. The blister, when opened, sometimes contains a brownish liquid with a chemical smell. We've heard rumors of blisters that were 4 inches across, and 1-inch blisters are common. Small fiberglass hulls are not very thick in places, so a blister that has soaked $\frac{1}{4}$ inch or $\frac{3}{8}$ inch into the hull could become a dangerous weakness if left undiscovered. A blister could weaken an area enough to allow it to be easily punctured.

Blistering may appear at any time, and once you find blisters on your boat, the chances are good that it'll blister again, assuming you do nothing about the overall problem. Bottom blistering doesn't occur in any one type or brand of hull. It happens in fresh and salt water, without regard to bottom paint type, and on boats left in the water year round as well as those hauled out periodically.

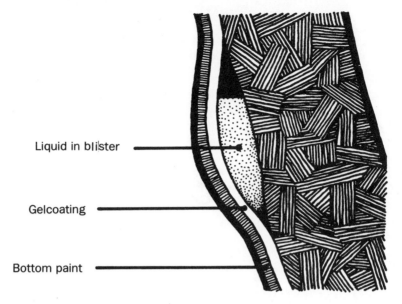

Section of a blister on fiberglass hull bottom.

What causes blistering? Some blame certain corrosive ingredients in polluted water. A more likely culprit is the quality of the polyester resin and the fiberglass cloth used for the laminate in combination with poor quality control during the lay-up procedure. The skill of the laminators, their ability to produce a properly catalyzed and well-mixed batch of resin, and to saturate the fiberglass cloth, mat and roving properly without leaving bubbles or voids is vital to the integrity of a fiberglass hull. Some blame the gelcoat itself, its ability to effectively seal the laminate underneath, or the way and condition in which it's applied to the mold. There are any number of opinions, none necessarily correct, but the preponderance of them points to the quality of materials and workmanship during layup as the prime suspects. Some boat owners feel the problem may be triggered or accelerated by sanding away part of the hull's original gelcoating when preparing for bottom paint, and that once this protective coating is scarred, the laminate beneath may be more vulnerable to water absorption.

If the laminator, at this critical first lamination stage, mixes a batch of resin too hot or with too little catalyst or should fail to properly roll out the lamination, thus leaving air bubbles or voids, or gets the gelcoat dirty before the glass is laid on, for instance, he could create the conditions for eventual osmosis. Simply put, the blister will try to equalize pressure by sucking water into itself from outside the hull, through the bottom paint and gelcoating.

Prevention and Cure

In our experience, the solution to bottom blistering is simple and may be expressed in one word — epoxy. Epoxy, an excellent moisture barrier when properly applied in sufficient depth, virtually stops the migration of water, offering a lasting repair and preventative treatment for fiberglass hull bottoms. Epoxy will not shrink or suffer from problems of water absorption like polyester-based repair materials. The blister treatments presently offered by manufacturers are for the most part epoxy-based.

The most commonly used method of preventing blisters is to sand well and apply a suitable thickness of epoxy resin to bare polyester laminate. Epoxy will also stick to clean, sanded, healthy gelcoat, so it may not

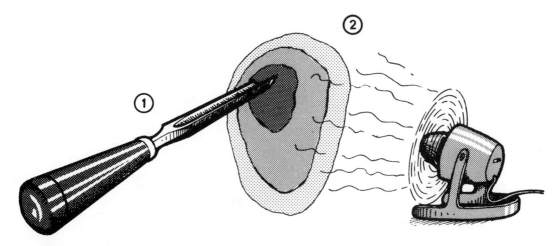

To repair fiberglass blisters:
1. Open up the blister by gouging and scrape back to dry the laminate.
2. Dry thoroughly with a fan. If necessary, use heat.

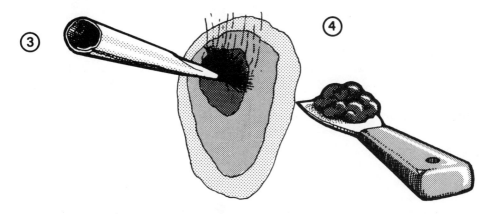

3. Using an acid brush, saturate the area with unthickened epoxy resin and let
    it kick.
4. Fill the area with a thick mixture of microballoons and epoxy.

always be necessary to remove all the gel-coating. The manufacturer of your epoxy and the boatbuilder can advise you as to the correct procedure.

The usual recommendation is for a minimum of three coats, or about 10 mils, in thickness, but five or six coats, or close to 20 mils, is much better for the additional protection. Sanding the entire bottom of the boat is a long and tedious process that requires a certain degree of skill and perseverance. It will also probably require some filling and fairing to achieve a good slick bottom after all that sanding.

Sandblasting is a good method for dealing with individual blisters. After they're cleaned out, they should be left to dry as long as possible, Depending somewhat on the weather and local climate, an electric heater and fans are good to help drying, and you can usually see the ring of moisture recede as it evaporates away. Heat lamps may also work well to speed the process.

For individual blisters, fill the cleaned

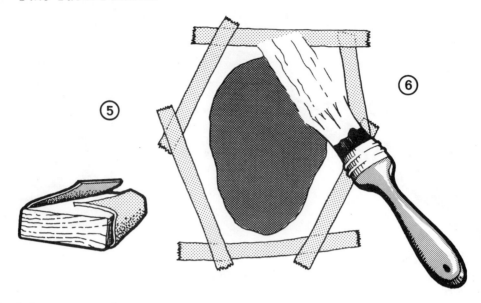

5. *Sand the area smooth.*
6. *Mask it off and paint.*

and dried depression with thickened epoxy, after first sealing the area with unthickened epoxy. Coat first with catalyzed epoxy, and for a filling and fairing compound, mix silica and microballoons with the epoxy and smear it on with a trowel, plastic squeegee, or wide putty knife. If the mixture will require extensive sanding, you'll want to use less silica, which is very dense and difficult to sand, and more microballoons. You could leave out the silica altogether, but it adds a degree of hardness and keeps the mixture from sagging.

If blisters appear in a great many places on the bottom of your boat, you may want to treat the entire surface. First, thoroughly sand or sandblast the hull and open all blisters. If the boat has been in salt water, wash it with fresh water and allow it to dry for several days. Roll a coating of epoxy onto the sanded area of the hull, and with a squeegee, apply a mixture of epoxy and microballoons to all the blister voids. After the hull cures, sand lightly, fair if necessary, and apply a final coat of epoxy. When the last coat of epoxy kicks, sand lightly again and apply bottom paint. In order to remove air bubbles created by the foam roller, follow the roller with a foam brush.

Appendix A

Fairing and Finishing External Lead Castings

In the past, we spent days fairing and smoothing plugs for lead ballast castings in hopes that they would come back from the foundry as smooth as glass. Some did, but some came back with numerous dings in the soft lead where the foundry or truckers had bumped them. It was something we had to live with; we filled and faired the best we could with polyester body putty, which always flaked off within a year or so, or the first time the boat went aground.

Epoxy has changed all that. In fact, when we build a lead casting plug we intentionally rough up the surface with a rasp. After the casting is bolted into place, we fair large dings by shaving away lead with a block plane; then we scrub the keel with solvent and roll on a coat of epoxy. Later, we spread

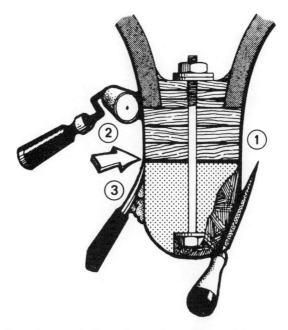

Fairing a lead casting — 1. Rough up the surface with a rasp or disc sander, clean shavings off, and degrease. 2. Coat with unthickened epoxy resin. 3. Apply a mixture of epoxy and microballoons, paying special attention to seam. Fair and sand for bottom painting.

119

the entire surface with a mixture of epoxy resin thickened with colloidal silica and microballoons. When this mixture kicks, we fair and sand with floats and blocks and finally by hand, then roll or brush on two coats of epoxy resin. After the epoxy has cured, we scrub down the surface with soap and water, and sand with 80- and 100-grit paper to make the plug ready for bottom paint. Epoxy sticks so well that we have never had a flaking problem; even when the boat has gone aground and gouged the lead, the epoxy coating has held up better than expected. We have never tried it, but the same treatment could possibly be used with an iron casting. It might be necessary to sandblast to get to a clean surface.

Appendix B

Estimates of Maximum Paint or Varnish Required for Two Coats Over a Sealed or Previously Primed Surface

Length of Boat	Topsides	Deck	Bottom
8-foot to 10-foot dinghy	1 quart		2 quarts
16-foot rowboat	2 quarts	1 quart	2 quarts
20-foot sailboat	1 gallon	2 quarts	1 gallon
25-foot sailboat	1½ gallons	1 gallon	2 gallons
30-foot motorboat	2½ gallons	1½ gallons	3 gallons
36-foot sailboat	2½ gallons	1½ gallons	3½ gallons

For new or bare surfaces, it is customary to double the quantities.

Enamel paint also requires slightly more quantity to cover the same area as polyurethane paint.

Appendix C

Product Field Report

by Ralph Naranjo

Before beginning a refinishing project, it's important to understand what products are available in the marketplace and how these products behave. The variety is enormous, and the consumer can easily be overwhelmed by the options available. The following look at what many boatyard professionals favor may help to clarify the situation.

Let's begin by looking at a few of the well-established players in the field: the major paint companies catering to the recreational boating market. International Paint's yacht division, Interlux, is the largest supplier of yacht finishes in the world. The company is more than 100 years old, and its products range from varnish and bottom paint to two-part polyurethanes. Koppers Co., Inc., has recently gathered three long-respected paint manufacturers, Pettit, Z*Spar, and Woolsey, under one umbrella. Z*Spar's yacht enamel—especially the clean glossy white—Pettit's bottom paint, and Woolsey's Blue Streak have remained industry favorites. Regatta, a Jotun company, with another 100-year-old reputation, markets one of the finest varnishes used in the industry.

Yacht maintenance has been revolutionized by the plastics industry, and the advent of high-tech coatings has spawned a variety of new entries in the marketplace. Premier examples of state-of-the-art products are Awlgrip and WEST System epoxies. Rather than generalize about such companies and their product lines, I will turn instead to specific products and the jobs that they do.

Bottom Paints

Paint manufacturers have spent years formulating compounds that are toxic to unwanted marine growth. Arsenic, mercury, and a few other unfriendly elements work quite well but have some nasty environmental side effects. Over the past 10 years, the industry has focused on copper and tin compounds for their action as toxicants. Copper, in the form of cuprous oxide, is an effective deterrent to marine growth. To some extent, the more metal suspended in the paint, the better the antifouling characteristics. The problem with these products in their original formulations, however, is that they are held in an inert binder, and once the surface loses its quality as a biocide, there is no significantly effective means of releasing the cuprous oxide trapped beneath the top layer.

The original tin paints worked in the same manner. Tributyltin (TBT) oxide, TBT fluoride, and TBT methacrylate are effective toxicants as they break down into tin oxide. But again, the antifouling qualities diminished as the surface wore. When Interlux introduced its Micron copolymer formula, the situation changed. Now the tin-compound toxicant and binder are linked in a chemical formula that hydrolyzes when in contact with seawater. This allows a more even leaching of the antifouling material. As long as there is paint on the surface, protection is provided. Vessels can be hauled, and later relaunched, without destroying the paint's antifouling capability, and the product provides an effective coating that lasts for more than one year.

Copolymer paints caught on quickly, despite their high per-gallon cost and the need to apply a thick coat, and many manufacturers now market them. Products such as Pettit Horizons and Z*Spar copolymer also perform well in this category.

As with many good products, there are also negatives. Those handling copolymers soon discovered that adverse reactions are common, so good handling procedures are a must. For safety, gloves, coveralls, and an organic vapor mask are commonsense precautions. Those who come home with as much paint on themselves as they leave on the boat are probably better off with a less toxic, more traditional bottom paint. Racing sailors will be pleased with the smooth surfaces associated with Micron, but those who choose to wet sand prior to launching should be careful to protect their arms and other exposed parts of their body from the wet residue. Spray painting should be left to the pros or those who thoroughly understand how to cope with the added danger of handling atomized coatings.

Other problems with TBT-based paints are emerging. Current research seems to indicate that if small concentrations are found in the water column, certain types of marine larvae, especially of shellfish, are adversely affected, so some states are enacting legislation to tightly control the sale of paints containing tin. At the moment, it is unclear whether or not free-associated (or encapsulated) as well as copolymer tin compounds will be affected. If the paint is deemed to be a harm to the environment and its sale controlled, copper-based paints will once again dominate the industry. Aluminum boat owners will face some serious concerns about electrolysis, and paint manufacturers will press their research and development facilities for new alternatives. Some manufacturers are taking a new look at non-toxic silicone paint. An improved product would prohibit marine growth on its slippery surface.

The terms *hard* and *soft* paint are now used less frequently, but consumers may still come across those designations as they shop for bottom paint. Vinyl paints—state-of-the-art 20 years ago—are a hard antifoulant. They adhere exceptionally well, but their antifouling protection tends to drop off rather abruptly as the season continues. They normally contain cuprous oxides, but a few also incorporate active tin ingredients. Excessive buildup of previous years' paint can be a problem with this type of coating.

Soft antifouling coats tend to slough away from the surface during the season. The buildup over years is not a problem, but too much enthusiasm in scrubbing the waterline can wipe paint completely from the surface. The new copolymers, which are a semisoft paint, incorporate the features that enhance both soft and hard bottom coats. They adhere well to the surface and tend not to be easily rubbed off.

Two-Part Polyurethanes

Awlgrip has set a standard in the industry. Seldom is there a product which so revolutionizes a trade that its brand name becomes the very name that describes the process. Most other major paint firms now produce an equivalent to Awlgrip. Suppliers may say it is "as good as Awlgrip." I've not heard any suggest that there is better. Imron, Interthane Plus, Durathane, and a host of other polyurethane paints have subsequently entered the marketplace.

Awlgrip and Imron are usually sprayed, placing them beyond the practical use of most consumers. Although it is impossible to brush them on, it is tricky and best left to professionals. Most paint companies, however, try to make the process as simple as possible. Interlux, for example, packages a brushable Interthane Plus with a complete list of procedures for the do-it-yourselfer; Durathane is another good brushable product.

Space-age polymers are effective, but there

WARNING: Make sure proper respiratory equipment is worn when sanding or spraying.

Company	Brand/List Price	Base/Toxicant	Colors	Compatible Hull Material/ Bottom Paints	Application/ Removal	Recoat/Launch (min.–max.)	Advertised Attributes
Baltic Marine Products, Inc. PO Box 14615 Chicago, IL 60614 (312) 645-0999	VC-17M/ $35.82-qt.	Teflon, fluorocarbon/Cu_2O metallic copper	Red, dk. navy, copper	W, FRP, Steel/hard paints only; chalking & eroding paints must be removed	Roller, spray/acetone	20 minutes/ min: immediately max: 1 year	Increases speed up to 10%. Will not cause paint buildup.
	VC-17 Tropicana/ $39.40-qt.	Teflon/Cu_2O	Red, dk. navy, copper	W, FRP, Steel/over hard paints only	Roller, spray/acetone	20 minutes/ min: immediately max: 1 year	For southern or other high-growth areas. Will not cause paint buildup.
Chilton Paint Company 109-09 15th Ave. College Point, NY 11356 (718) 359-0438	Chilton "Dripless" Red or Blue Copper/$66-gal.	Rosin/Cu_2O	Red, blue	W, FRP, Al/over most other paints except bronze	Brush, roller/sanding	12 hrs/ min: none max: 3 days	Paints on heavy. Safe from drips.
	Chilton "Standard" $53.50-gal.	Rosin/	Red	W, FRP, Al/over most other paints except bronze	Brush, roller/sanding	12 hrs/ min: none max: 3 days	Good grade antifoulant designed for commercial boats.
Dyco Chemicals & Coatings, Inc. 5850 Ulmerton Rd. Clearwater, FL 33520-3989 (800) 237-8232 (800) 282-7901 in FL	Biomax 610/ $98.00-gal.	Copolymer/TBTO*	Clear, white, brown, blue, red	FRP, Steel, Al/only over other hard finishes	Brush, roller, spray/ sanding or paint remover	4 hrs/ min: 18 hrs max: 90 days	Completely clear finish, Lasts 2 yrs. Increases efficiency. Must be used with 700 Clear Primer. ($36.00-gal)
International Paint Co., Inc. 2270 Morris Ave. Union, NJ 07083 (800) INTRLUX (201) 686-1300 in NJ	Micron 33/ $175-gal.	Tin based copolymer/ TBTF*	Red, blue, blk, white, green, brown	W, FRP, Steel, Al/over vinyl, hard epoxy esters & copolymers only	Brush, roller, spray/ Pint-Off #199 over wood, Pint-Off #299 over FRP; will not harm gelcoat	overnight/ min: overnight max: unlimited	Copolymer for multiseason protection; smooth, hard finish for racing sailors. Surface can be burnished for drysailed, rack-stored, & trailered boats. Thin 10% over wood.
	Clear 25/ $48.95-qt.	Tin based copolymer/ TBTF*	Clear	W, FRP/over copolymers & enamels only	Brush, roller/ See Micron 33	overnight/ min: overnight max: unlimited	Ideal for bootop & splash areas. Copolymer. Fast polishing, high strength.
	Copper-Lux/ $146.25-gal.	Epoxy resin/ Cu_2O	Red, blue, blk green, brown	W, FRP, Steel/over most bottom paints	Brush, roller/See Micron 33, or sand	overnight/ min: overnight max: 72 hrs	For severe fouling in tropical waters. Use barrier coat over steel hulls before painting.

Key: Cu_2O - Cuprous Oxide; TBTO - Tributyltin Oxide; TBTF - Tributyltin Fluoride; TBTF - Tributyltin Methacrylate; TBTA - Tributyltin Adipate; TBTM - Tributyltin Methacrylate; W - wood; FRP - fiberglass; Al - aluminum.

*Several states, France, and England are enacting legislation to control or ban sale and use of TBT-based paint.

(Compiled by *Small Boat Journal*, Bennington, VT. Copyright 1987)

Company	Brand/List Price	Base/Toxicant	Colors	Compatible Hull Material/ Bottom Paints	Application/ Removal	Recoat/Launch (min.–max.)	Advertised Attributes
International Paint Co., Inc.	Super Bottomkote/ $117.95-gal.	Modified Epoxy Resin/ Cu_2O	Red, blue, blk, green, brown	W, FRP, Steel/over most bottom paints	Brush, roller, spray/ *See Micron 33*	overnight/ min: overnight max: 60 days	For southern waters & unrelenting marine growth. Long-term, in-water service; 12–15 months.
	Fiberglass Bottomkote/ $108.45-gal.	Modified Epoxy Ester/ Cu_2O	Red, blue, green, blk, brown, bronze	W, FRP, Steel/over all bottom paints	Brush, roller, spray/ *See Micron 33*	overnight/ min: overnight max: 60 days	Long-term protection. Smooth, hard finish.
	Bottomkote/ $87.95-gal.	Rosin/Cu_2O	Red, green, blue	W, FRP, Steel/ over all bottom paints	Brush, roller, spray/ *See Micron 33*	overnight/ min: overnight max: 48 hrs	Suitable for cruising boats. Slowly eroding soft film.
	#999 Fiberglass Bottomkote/ $108.45-gal.	Modified Epoxy/ Cu_2O	Bronze	W, FRP/over all hard bottom paints	Brush, roller, spray/ *See Micron 33*	2–3 hrs/ min: overnight max: 60 days	Inland waters. Smooth, hard racing finish.
	Super Viny-Lux/ $125.95-gal.	Vinyl/Cu_2O	Red, blue	W, FRP, Steel/only over other vinyl paints	Brush, roller, spray/ *See Micron 33*	5 hrs/ min: overnight max: 60 days	Full-season durability. Easier brushing.
	Viny-Lux/ $104.95-gal.	Vinyl resin/Cu_2O	Red, blue, green	W, FRP, Steel/only over other vinyl paints	Brush, roller, spray/ *See Micron 33*	5 hrs/ min: overnight max: 60 days	Hard, abrasion-resistant finish.
	Tri-Lux/ $129.45-gal.	Vinyl/TBTF*	Red, lt blue, dk green, dk blue, blk, white	W, FRP, Al/only over other vinyl paints	Brush, roller, spray/ *See Micron 33*	overnight/ min: overnight max: 3 months	Inland waters. For racing/cruising sailboats & trailerable boats. Smooth, hard racing finish w/superior abrasion resistance. Will not cause galvanic action when used over aluminum.
	Supertrop/ $79.95-gal.	Rosin/Cu_2O	Red, blue	W, FRP, Steel/over all bottom paints	Brush, roller, spray/ *See Micron 33*	overnight/ min: overnight max: 48 hrs	General purpose soft film & fast leaching.
	Red Hand/ $59.95-gal.	Rosin/Cu_2O	Red, blue, green	W, FRP/ over all bottom paints	Brush, roller, spray/ *See Micron 33*	overnight/ min: overnight max: 48 hrs	Season-long performance in less temperate waters. Recommended for commercial fishermen.

Company	Brand/List Price	Base/Toxicant	Colors	Compatible Hull Material/ Bottom Paints	Application/ Removal	Recoat/Launch (min.–max.)	Advertised Attributes
International Paint Co., Inc.	62T Anti-fouling/ $81.35-gal.	Vinyl/Cu$_2$O	Red, blue	W, FRP, Steel/over all bottom paints	Brush, roller, spray/ *See* Micron 33	4 hrs/ min: 2 hrs max: 48 hrs	Developed for West Coast waters. Soft film & fast leaching.
	Micron 44/ $184.95-gal.	Copolymer/ Cu$_2$O, tin	Red, blue, green, blk, brown	W, FRP, Steel/only over other vinyls, hard epoxy esters & copolymers	Brush, roller, spray/ *See* Micron 33	overnight/ min: overnight max: unlimited	Copolymer. For cruising sailboats & fast sport fishing powerboats in heavy slime areas.
ITW Philadelphia Resins Corp. PO Box 454 Montgomeryville, PA 18936 (215) 855-8450	Classic Yacht/ $209-gal.	Hydrophobic polymer/Biocidal organo-metallic polymer	Clear, red, blue, blk, white, brown	W, FRP, Al, Steel/ only over other vinyls & epoxy esters	Brush, spray/	1 hr/ min: 6 hrs max: unlimited	For racing & cruising boats, commercial vessels in fresh and salt water. Two-year protection. Smooth, slippery, low-friction surface.
Koppers Company, Inc. 1328 Koppers Bldg. Pittsburgh, PA 15219 (412) 227-2000	Z•Spar Vinyl Cup/ $107-gal.	Vinyl rosin/Cu$_2$O	Red, blue, green	W, FRP, Steel/only over vinyl type paints	Brush, roller, spray/ sanding	3 hrs/ min: 3 hrs max: 7 days	Hard racing finish for power & sail. Excellent for wood and fiberglass. Use barrier coat over steel hulls before painting.
	Supertox Anti-fouling/ $112.95-gal.	Modified epoxy ester/Cu$_2$O, organotin	Red, blue, blk, brown	W, FRP, Steel/only over hard antifouling	Brush, roller, spray/ sanding	4 hrs/ min: 6 hrs max: 7 days	Hard racing finish for power & sail. Excellent for wood and fiberglass. Use barrier coat over steel hulls before painting.
	The Protector/ $150-gal.	Epoxy ester & hard resin, epoxy-resin/ Cu$_2$O	Red, blue	W, FRP, Steel/only over hard antifouling paints	Brush, roller, spray/ sanding	4 hrs/ min: overnight max: 7 days	Hard finish for boats with high-speed capabilities or craft that operate in heavy fouling waters. Contains more copper than other paints by this manufacturer.
	Colortox/ $113-gal.	Vinyl-rosin/ organotin	Red, blue, blk, green, white	W, FRP, Steel, Al/only over vinyl-type paints	Brush, roller/	3 hrs/ min: 18 hrs max: 30 days	Hard, smooth surface. Does not cause galvanizing action. Ideal for steel & aluminum hulls. Racing boats.
	Multitox/ $95.50-gal.	Epoxy rosin/Cu$_2$O	Red, blue	W, FRP, Steel/only over hard antifouling paints	Brush, roller/ sanding	4 hrs. min: 6 hrs max: 7 days	Semi-soft type for salt or fresh water. Used on oceangoing vessels & pleasure boats with high-speed capabilities to 18 knots.
	3010 Coppertox Anti-fouling paint (East coast)/ $60.75-gal.	Rosin/Cu$_2$O	Red	W, FRP, Steel, Al/over most old bottom paints	Brush, roller/	4 hrs/ min: 6 hrs max: 7 days	Semi-soft. Designed for the budget-minded yachtsman. For slow-moving commercial boats not exceeding 18 knots.

Key: Cu$_2$O - Cuprous Oxide; TBTO - Tributyltin Oxide; TBTF - Tributyltin Fluoride; TBTA - Tributyltin Adipate; TBTM - Tributyltin Methacrylate; W - wood; FRP - fiberglass; Al - aluminum.

*Several states, France, and England are enacting legislation to control or ban sale and use of TBT-based paint.

(Compiled by *Small Boat Journal*, Bennington, VT. Copyright 1987)

Company	Brand/List Price	Base/Toxicant	Colors	Compatible Hull Material/Bottom Paints	Application/Removal	Recoat/Launch (min.-max.)	Advertised Attributes
Koppers Company Inc.	2000 Anti-fouling paint (West coast)/ $73.30-gal.	Rosin/Cu_2O	Red oxide	W, FRP, Steel, Al/over most old bottom paints	Brush, roller/	2 hrs/ min: 2 hrs max: 12 days	Semi-soft for fresh or salt water. Protects wood hulls against borers.
	B-60 Racing Bronze/ $112.50-gal.	Rosin/Copper powder organotin	Bronze	W, FRP/over most old paints	Brush, roller/	4 hrs/ min: 4 hrs max: 7 days	Hard coating designed for racing hulls for use in salt & fresh water. Contains high percentage of pure metal flakes.
Pettit Paint Company, Inc. 36 Pine St. Rockaway, NJ 07866 (201) 625-3100	Unepoxy/ $72.50–141.95-gal.	Epoxy-rosin/ TBTO, Cu_2O*	Red, blue, blk, green, bronze, white	W, FRP, Steel/over all hard bottom paints	Brush, roller, spray/ heat, sanding, paint or varnish remover	4 hrs/ min: 8 hrs max: 2 months	Excellent protection, hard, modified epoxy. Tropic, Atlantic, Pacific, Inland. Regionally formulated.
	Trinidad 75/ $139.95-gal.	Epoxy rosin/Cu_2O	Red, blue, blk, brown	W, FRP, Steel/over all hard bottom paints	Brush, roller, spray/ heat, sanding, paint or varnish remover	4 hrs/ min: 8 hrs max: 2 months	Excellent protection, hard, modified epoxy. For competitive racing or bluewater cruising; year-round service.
	Horizons/ $165-gal.	Acrylic-copolymer/ TBTM, Cu_2O*	Red, blue, blk, green, brown	W, FRP, Steel/only over hard antifouling paints	Brush, roller, spray/ heat, sanding, paint or varnish remover	4 hrs/ min: 8 hrs max: unlimited	Best protection, multiseasonal. Copolymer. Semi-hard; slow to moderate speed boats in cool waters.
	Hard Horizons/ $179-gal.	Acrylic-copolymer/ TBTM, Cu_2O*	Red, blue, blk, green, brown	W, FRP, Steel/only over hard antifouling paints	Brush, roller, spray/ heat, sanding, paint or varnish remover	4 hrs/ min: 8 hrs max: unlimited	Hard; fast (above 25 knots) boats & sport fishermen in warm tropical waters.
	Yacht Copper Red, Green/$53.95-gal.- green, $49.95-red	Rosin/Cu_2O	Red, green	W, FRP, Steel/over all soft & hard bottom paints	Brush, roller, spray/ heat, sanding, paint or varnish remover	16 hrs/ min: 8 hrs max: 48 hrs	Visibly indicates when it's time to repaint. No old coating buildup.
	Starline Bronze/ $87.60-gal.	Acrylic rosin/ TBTO & copper powder*	Bronze	W, FRP/over all soft & hard bottom paints	Brush, roller, spray/ heat, sanding, paint or varnish remover	4 hrs/ min: 6 hrs max: 2 months	For inland lakes or fresh water.
	Tropicop/ $71.30-gal. $85.60-gal.-blue & green	Rosin/Cu_2O	Red, green, blue	W, Steel/over all soft & hard bottom paints	Brush, roller, spray/ heat, sanding, paint or varnish remover	6 hrs/ min: 6 hrs max: 2 months	Good protection. Semi-hard.
	Alumaguard/ $121.30-gal.	Vinyl-rosin/ TBTA*	Red, blue, blk, green, white	W, Steel, Al/only over vinyl based paints. Remove all others.	Brush, roller, spray/ heat, sanding, paint or varnish remover	4 hrs/ min: 16 hrs max: unlimited	Strong protection.

Company	Brand/List Price	Base/Toxicant	Colors	Compatible Hull Material/ Bottom Paints	Application/ Removal	Recoat/Launch (min.-max.)	Advertised Attributes
Pettit Paint Company, Inc.	Bioguard/ $116.95-gal.	Vinyl-rosin/ TBTA*	Red, blue, blk, green, white	W, FRP, Steel/only over vinyl based paints	Brush, roller, spray/ heat, sanding, paint or varnish remover	4 hrs/ min: 16 hrs max: unlimited	Strong protection.
	Yacht Copper Special Red or Blue/$53.95-gal.	Rosin/Cu₂O	Red, blue	W/over all paints	Brush, roller, spray/ heat, sanding, paint or varnish remover	16 hrs/ min: 8 hrs max: 24 hrs	Over slow-moving wooden boats in fresh or salt water.
	Anti-Fouling Copper Bronze/ $111.95-gal.	Rosin/copper powder	Copper bronze	W/over any hard or soft paints	Brush, roller, spray/ heat, sanding, paint or varnish remover	4 hrs/ min: 6 hrs max: 24 hrs	Over slow-moving wooden boats in fresh or salt water.
	Vinylcide Red/Blue $104.95-gal.	Vinyl-rosin/Cu₂O	Red, blue	W, Steel/only over vinyl based paints	Brush, roller, spray/ heat, sanding, paint or varnish remover	4 hrs/ min: 4 hrs max: 2 months	Hard finish for fast boats.
Regatta Marine Coatings, Inc. 175 Penrod Ct. Glen Burnie, MD 21061 (301) 761-8877	Baltoguard/ $132.95-gal.	Chlorinated Rubber/ Cu₂O, TBTF*	Red, blue	W, FRP, Steel/over most old coatings, but not over soft commercial antifoulings	Spray, roller, brush/ sanding	4-6 hrs/ min: 6 hrs max: 2 weeks	Extremely durable coating for effective long periods between haulouts. Hard finish suited for oceangoing ships, yachts & commercial vessels
	Baltoplate/ $165-gal.	Vinyl/Cu₂O	Metallic gunmetal	W, FRP, Steel, Al/only over vinyl-type paints containing cuprous oxide	Spray, brush/sanding	overnight/ min: overnight max: unlimited	Extremely hard finish that may be burnished with bronze wool and maintained at a level of smoothness equal to that of polished metal. Good choice for boats stored on a trailer.
Rule Industries, Inc. Cape Ann Industrial Park Gloucester, MA 01930 (617) 281-0440	KL-990 Komposition/ $103.50-gal.	Organic bound copper/Cu₂O	Red, blue, blk, green, brown	W, FRP, Steel/over existing coatings	Brush, spray/sanding, paint or varnish remover	overnight/ min: overnight max: 1 year	For salt & fresh water. 12-month life; long-wearing against barnacles.
	KL-990 Polycop/ $129.50-gal.	Rosin/Cu₂O, copper tin	Red, blue	W, FRP, Steel/over existing coatings	Brush, roller, spray/ sanding, paint or varnish remover	overnight/ min: overnight max: 1 year	Protects against all marine growths; 18-month life.
	KL-990 Graph-Cote/ $119-gal.	Rosin/Cu₂O, copper tin	Gray	W, FRP, Steel/over existing coatings	Brush, roller, spray/ sanding, paint or varnish remover	overnight/ min: overnight max: 1 year	For serious racers. Friction-resistant graphite. Burnishing.

Key: Cu₂O - Cuprous Oxide; TBTO - Tributyltin Oxide; TBTF - Tributyltin Fluoride; TBTA - Tributyltin Adipate; TBTM - Tributyltin Methacrylate; W - wood; FRP - fiberglass; Al - aluminum.

*Several states, France, and England are enacting legislation to control or ban sale and use of TBT-based paint.

(Compiled by *Small Boat Journal*, Bennington, VT. Copyright 1987)

Company	Brand/List Price	Base/Toxicant	Colors	Compatible Hull Material/ Bottom Paints	Application/ Removal	Recoat/Launch (min.–max.)	Advertised Attributes
Rule Industries, Inc.	KL-990 Graph-Cup/ $129.50-gal.	Rosin/Cu_2O, copper tin	Brown	W, FRP, Steel/over existing coatings	Brush, roller, spray/ sanding, paint or varnish remover	overnight/ min: overnight max: 1 year	Same as Polycop but extra antifouling.
	KL-990 Super Epoxy/$115-gal.	Epoxy-Rosin/ Cu_2O, tin	Red, blue, brown, blk	W, FRP, Steel/only over hard paints	Brush, roller, spray/ sanding, paint or varnish remover	overnight/ min: overnight max: 1 year	For high- and low-speed boats.
	KL-990 Fresh Water/$64.95-gal.	Copolymer/	White	W, FRP, Al/	Brush, roller, spray/	overnight/	Product for fresh water. Contains no copper.
Specialty Marine Coatings Box 898 Fayetteville, TN 37334 (615) 433-1573	Formula 7/ $120-gal.	Epoxy/Cu_2O	Red, blue, blk, gray	W, FRP, Al, Steel/over all previous paints	Brush, roller, spray/ sanding	15 minutes/ min: overnight max: 48 hrs	Easy application. Sands easily. Smooth finish for racing boats. Use barrier coat over steel & aluminum hulls.
	Formula 15/ $120-gal.	Vinyl/Cu_2O	Red, blk	W, FRP/over all previous paints	Brush, roller, spray/ solvent-based paint remover	15 min/ min: overnight max: 48 hrs	Soft sloughing type for slower moving cruising boats. Great antifoulant. Use barrier coat over steel & aluminum hulls.
U.S. Paint, Div. of Grow Group Inc. 831 S. 21st St. St. Louis, MO 63103 (314) 621-0525	Awlgrip Awlstar Goldlabel 73113 red, 73114 blue, 73115 blk./$169-gal.	Polypeptide polymer/Cu_2O	Red, blue, blk	W, FRP, Steel/old coatings except vinyl; recommends removal of old coating	Brush, roller, spray/ sanding	4 hrs/ min: 5 hrs max: unlimited	Self-polishing surface; for serious fouling & extended drydocking intervals. Multiseason use. Tin free.
	Awlgrip Awlstar Blue Label 73134 red, 73132 blk, 73133 lt blue/ $155.34-gal.	Ablative polypeptide polymer/Cu_2O, TBT*	Red, lt blue, blk	W, FRP, Steel/Will not work over tin copolymers or soft conventional types; should work over hard conventional types	Brush, roller, spray/ sanding	4 hrs/ min: 5 hrs max: unlimited	For West Coast waters; ideal for serious fouling conditions and for extended drydocking intervals. Multiple seasons.
Valspar Corp. PO Box 625 Raritan, NJ 08869-0625 (800) 258-4455 (201) 725-8800 in NJ	Red Copper Anti-Fouling Bottom Paint/$69.99-gal.	Pine tar/Cu_2O	Red copper	W, FRP, Al, Steel/only over old surface in good condition	Brush, roller/sanding or Valspar Marine Stripper	12 hrs/ min: 24 hrs max: 48 hrs	Low-cost fresh water antifouling protection. Not for use on boats that are trailered or removed from water longer than 48 hours. Do not apply to bare metal.
	Hi Performance Red Copper A/F Bottom Paint/ $129.99-gal.	Tar/Cu_2O	Red copper	W, FRP, Al, Steel/only over old surface in good condition	Brush, spray/sanding or Valspar Marine Stripper	12 hrs/ min: 4 hrs max: 48 hrs	For use in ocean including heavy fouling tropic areas. Do not apply to bare metal.

Company	Brand/List Price	Base/Toxicant	Colors	Compatible Hull Material/Bottom Paints	Application/Removal	Recoat/Launch (min.-max.)	Advertised Attributes
Valspar Corp.	Escolux Bronze Anti-Fouling Bottom Paint/ $82.99-gal.	Cu₂O	Bronze	W, FRP, Al, Steel/only over old surface in good condition	Brush, spray/sanding or Valspar Marine Stripper	6 hrs/ min: 48 hrs max: 1 week	Ideal for use in fresh water in temperate climates. Do no apply to bare metal.
	Vinyl Anti-Fouling Bottom Paint/ $89.99-gal.	Vinyl/Cu₂O	Red, blue, blk	W, FRP, Al, Steel/only over old surface in good condition	Brush, spray/sanding or Valspar Marine Stripper	8 hrs/ min: 48 hrs max: 48 hrs	For maximum antifouling action. Yearly maintenance is suggested.
Woolsey Marine Paints, Div. of Koppers, Inc. 480 Freylinghuysen Ave., Newark, NJ 07114 (201) 824-9000	Tradewinds/ $92.50-gal.	Rosin/Cu₂O	Red, blue, green, brown, bronze	W, FRP, Metal/over all previous coatings	Brush, spray/ Woolsey 433 Thinner	3 hrs/ min: 4 hrs max: 72 hrs	For slower moving craft.
	Seamate/ $57.50-gal. $67.50-gal. blue	Rosin/Cu₂O	Red, blue	W/over all previous coatings	Brush, spray/ Woolsey 433 Thinner	5 hrs/ min: 6 hrs max: 7 days	Soft, sloughing type; season-long protection.
	Miracol/ $183.75-gal.	Acrylic-copolymer/ tin	Red, blue, blk, green, white	W, FRP, metal, Al/over other antifouling paints	Brush, spray/ Woolsey 433 Thinner	6 hrs/ min: 16 hrs max: unlimited	Self-polishing multiyear copolymer.
	Neptune/ $149.95-gal.	Epoxy-rosin/ Cu₂O	Red, blue, blk, brown, green	W, FRP/over all previous coatings	Brush, roller, spray/ Woolsey 433 Thinner	6 hrs/ min: 6 hrs max: 7 days	Maximum protection in heaviest fouling waters.
	Blue Streak/ $144.95-gal.	Epoxy-rosin/ Cu₂O	Blue	W, FRP/over all old finishes	Brush, roller, spray/ Woolsey 433 Thinner	6 hrs/ min: 6 hrs max: 7 days	Speed coating with film-forming surface. Hard racing finish.
	Queen of the Seas/ $99.95-gal.	Metal resinate modified epoxy/ Cu₂O	Red, blue, blk	W, FRP, metal/over most antifoulants	Brush, roller, spray/ Woolsey 433 Thinner	6 hrs/ min: 8 hrs max: 1 week	Smooth bottom for racing craft.
	Maxitox/ $104.95-gal.	Epoxy-rosin/ Cu₂O	Red, blue, blk, brown	W, FRP, metal/over most antifoulants	Brush, roller, spray/ Woolsey 433 Thinner	3 hrs/ min: 8 hrs max: 1 week	Acrylic base antifouling paint for wood

Key: Cu₂O - Cuprous Oxide; TBTO - Tributyltin Oxide; TBTF - Tributyltin Fluoride; TBTA - Tributyltin Adipate; TBTM - Tributyltin Methacrylate; W - wood; FRP - fiberglass; Al - aluminum.

*Several states, France, and England are enacting legislation to control or ban sale and use of TBT-based paint.

(Compiled by *Small Boat Journal*, Bennington, VT. Copyright 1987)

Company	Brand/List Price	Base/Toxicant	Colors	Compatible Hull Material/ Bottom Paints	Application/ Removal	Recoat/Launch (min.–max.)	Advertised Attributes
Woolsey Marine Paints	Super Vinelast/ $127.95-gal.	Vinyl-rosin/ Cu_2O	Red, blue, brown, green	W, FRP, metal/over any good surface	Brush, roller, spray/ Woolsey 433 Thinner	1 hr/ min: overnight max: 72 hrs	Tough, slime-resistant formula for slow or high-speed hulls.
	Vinelast/ $118.50-gal.	Vinyl-rosin/ Cu_2O	Red, blue, brown, green	W, FRP, metal/over any good surface. Only over other vinyls.	Brush, roller, spray/ Woolsey 483 Thinner	1 hr/ min: overnight max: 72 hrs	Hard, smooth surface; ideal for trailering.
	Lumalast/ $124.95-gal.	Vinyl-rosin/ tin	Red, blue, blk, green, white	W, FRP, Al/over all old finishes	Brush, roller, spray/ Woolsey 483 Thinner	4 hrs/ min: overnight max: unlimited	No galvanic action.

Key: Cu_2O - Cuprous Oxide; TBTO - Tributyltin Oxide; TBTF - Tributyltin Fluoride; TBTA - Tributyltin Adipate; TBTM - Tributyltin Methacrylate; W - wood; FRP - fiberglass; Al - aluminum.

*Several states, France, and England are enacting legislation to control or ban sale and use of TBT-based paint.

(Compiled by *Small Boat Journal*, Bennington, VT. Copyright 1987)

is a flip side. These products present a safety concern as well as tending to be more difficult to handle than conventional alkyd enamel. Time and time again I have watched a good do-it-yourself brush handler, accustomed to alkyd enamels and spar varnish, get into serious trouble with polyurethane paint. The problems usually stem from not following the manufacturer's explicit directions. The chemistry of these products requires specific mixing ratios. The person who forgets to purchase the manufacturer's brushing reducer and decides to simply use a little mineral spirits and Penetrol—as he does with all his other paints—is in for a big surprise. So is the chap who fails to add the proper amount of converter to the basecoat color.

The remainder of the project will hinge on the quality of the preparatory work, the skill of the applicator, the luck one has with the weather, insect populations, and neighbors in the boatyard who decide to do some serious sanding.

Traditional Alkyd Enamels

Oil-based enamels are unquestionably easier to work with than polyurethanes. Without a doubt they are less toxic and can, if applied correctly, provide an enviable finish. However, they don't last well. Top-notch conventional yacht enamels, such as Z*Spar #100, look brilliant the season they are applied, and if the preparation and buildup are good, they may even last a second season. After that, they chalk, and their adhesive qualities deteriorate rapidly. The Awlgrip advocate will point to 5-year-old paint jobs that still retain much of their original "wet look." Those who opt for conventional enamels see annual painting as part of the boating routine. If they hire a yard to do a first-class job, cost-effective decision-making may say that a two-part polyurethane paint is really a better way to go.

Neither conventional enamels nor Awlgrip can sustain serious abrasion from unpadded surfaces. One pass by a dock with a few nailheads protruding above the surface can cause a very expensive paint job to be ruined.

In situations where abrasion is a fact of life, conventional enamel paint and annual re-coating may be the best alternative after all. It can be touched up with less trouble, and the initial capital investment is significantly less.

A halfway high-tech approach may be the best of do-it-yourself alternatives. One-part modified alkyd enamels are a good choice in marine paints. Interlux Interpoly is an oil-modified polyurethane that flows smoothly, offers good hiding capabilities, and has much better abrasion resistance than a straight alkyd enamel. Easypoxy by Pettit and Monopoxy by Z*Spar are additional examples of one-part modified coatings. These products are not quite the thoroughbred of a two-part polyurethane coating. They will outlast conventional alkyd enamels, however, and are equally as easy to handle.

Varnishes

A flawlessly finished piece of hardwood draws attention. The do-it-yourselfer thinks of the demands in coats, hours, and pieces of sandpaper. Yesterday's yachtsman thinks of his granddad's schooner and how handy it was to have help around to attend to the brightwork chores. Today it's a different boating world. Varnish brushes are in the hands of many boat owners, and quite a few of them do a good job. Time, patience, and a good badger-hair brush lead the list of prerequisites. Shortcuts such as quick-dry varnish tend to catch up with the applicator in the end. The softer spar varnishes are still around but, like alkyd enamels, many have been polymerized.

One-part polyurethanes seem to be cutting into the traditional tung oil market. Recently Epifanes, a product from Holland, has become a popular brightwork coating. It provides excellent gloss as well as long-lasting durability. On the domestic scene, Regatta #3105 has proven to be a good choice. My own experiences with Z*Spar, Captains #1015, and Interlux #97 as well as its #96 Schooner Varnish (UV) have been good. These products flow well, sand smoothly, and tend to be stable in ultraviolet light.

Cross-linking polymers (two-part polyurethanes) with UV stabilizers are available in clear versions. Epoxy basecoats followed by several clear coats of polyurethane material can replace conventional varnish. Interthane plus clear or other similar polyurethane products can provide a finish that is as smooth as glass and equally transparent. It will outlast any conventional varnish. The drawbacks are twofold. First of all, the preparation work to achieve such a finish is lengthy and exacting. And second, when it comes to finally coping with the surface when it does need renewing, one wishes he were facing conventional varnish. These products are more resistant to varnish remover, and much harder to sand and scrape. They are difficult to feather-in and repair. What is gained in gloss and longevity may have to be paid back when it comes time to wood the surface.

Sealers

Teak coatings other than varnish abound. The claims of their manufacturers are, let's say, optimistic. The fact of the matter is simple. Teak, like any other wood, will react with oxygen and the chemicals in the environment it is exposed to. Fortunately teak is a resin-rich hardwood that withstands weathering better than other, similar species. Eventually, however, the smooth, honey-colored surface will change to a silver gray. As time goes on, the wood darkens and the softer part of the grain is eroded away. Glue joints may separate, and the wood can check and crack. Keeping the surface coated can prevent such deterioration. The object of sealers is to provide a thin film that will inhibit the chemical change. Most products soak into the timber as well as remain on the surface. They tend to require regular recoating (several times a season), but the detail involved is much simpler than varnishing. Deks Olje remains a favorite of the anti-varnish group. It's a product of the Flood Company and comes in mat and glossy. If several coats of the mat finish are put on well-cleaned and sanded wood, and this is followed by two or three coats of gloss finish, a reasonably durable and attractive coating is produced. Near the latter part of the summer a coat or two of the mat product will revitalize

the tired surface. Supporters of this process say that it doesn't require the Michelangelo brush techniques attributed to good varnish work. Coats can be applied more quickly, and the final results attained sooner. Skeptics say, "Tie up next to an old Alden schooner with a properly varnished toerail and compare it with the sealer system." There is no question that 11 coats of meticulously applied varnish make a piece of teak or mahogany look like a furniture showroom masterpiece, but boats don't sit in the living room, and winch handles and anchor flukes have been known to test the impact resistance of various brightwork coatings. You will have to decide what your finish level demands will be and choose products accordingly.

I regularly use Teak Wonder, a dressing sealer marketed by T-Jett Enterprises, Inc. It is not a miracle finish that eliminates all drudgery, but it does yield a warm honey-colored finish that seems to outlast most of the other sealers. I try to avoid overly viscous oils, which tend to turn into a dark gummy residue by the end of the season. Epifanes, the Dutch varnish manufacturer, also has a wood finish that is very appropriate for teak. There is no need to sand between coats as long as there is less than a 72-hour delay between applications. It is a hard glossy finish, which seems to be halfway between a varnish and an average sealer. This coating seems to last longer than others I have used and is worth a try. Remember to keep all these products on the wood where they belong and off gelcoat or polyurethane coatings. All too often, drips and spills are not noticed initially. After a week or two, it's hard not to see the discolored runs streaming away from the over-energetically coated woodwork. Good cosmetic attention during the application phase can keep this from becoming a problem. I like to keep a bottle of nonabrasive spray cleaner and a roll of paper towels handy. Any runs or drips get wiped up immediately.

Epoxy

The resin of the century can be a laminate, a glue, a filler paste, or a paint. WEST System has hit the target in its efforts to provide the boating community with a versatile product. Its approach has been to provide a basic resin with a "salad bar" full of additives that slightly change its properties in order to better suit a specific situation. For building and parts fabrication, their materials receive the nod of the industry. WEST System epoxy is a sound product with good technical information available from the manufacturer.

When it comes to cosmetic work prior to a polyurethane top coat, most builders turn to Interlux or Awlgrip for a complete line of ready-made putties and primers. These materials vary in consistency and durability. For example, a "high build" primer such as Awlquick is the choice of many pros, because of its ability to cover and its easy sanding characteristics. Unfortunately, it is not as good an adhesive as Awlgrip #545 or Interlux's #404/414 Barrier Kote. Therefore, the applicator must know what demands are to be placed upon the product before the choice is made. Manufacturers provide product data sheets; be sure to look these over.

Epoxy paint can be used as an undercoater or primer. Its abrasion resistance and adhesive qualities are superb. Unfortunately, it possesses very little ultraviolet light stability and quickly chalks when utilized as a top coating. Consequently it is at its best when used to tie a polyurethane coating to the hull material underneath.

Most boatyards specializing in exotic spray-paint work agree that epoxy-paste fairing products may be harder to sand than their polyester counterparts, but they do last longer, are less likely to soak up water, and stick far better. Those doing repairs to underwater surfaces see Pettit's Polypoxy, Interlux's #417A/418B, and Marinetex as better alternatives to Bondo-type polyester autobody fillers. Interlux also makes a high-solids epoxy paint, formulated as an effective underwater coating. It has proven to be quite useful as a repair product for bottom blistering. Interprotect #1000/1001 and Interprotect #2000/2001 are applied to a well-sanded filled and faired surface. The #1000 product is basically a pure laminating resin and is suggested to be used on areas where fiber material of the hull is visible. The #2000 product is used to provide a new hull skin with a rather impervious nature. The handling characteristics of the coating are good and the direct no-sanding recoatability of the #2000 Interprotect is advantageous. Pettit offers a bottom blister repair combination of its own, recommending #7020/7025 fairing compound followed by several coats of #4171 epoxy undercoater. The industry consensus of the process is to: open blisters, flush residue, dry the hull as much as possible, fill voids with epoxy, and overcoat with as impervious a coating as possible.

Adhesives and Sealants

Water has a way of getting into where it doesn't belong. Deck hardware, improperly bedded during installation, tends to be the biggest cause of below-deck leaks. A variety of manufacturers provide space-age products formulated to stop the drips. We can divide them into three major groups: polysulfides, silicones, and polyurethanes.

The polysulfides, such as Boatlife's Life Caulk, 3M's #101 and similar one-part flexible sealants, all smell like bad eggs while you work with them, but they do their job admirably. Life Caulk is a good choice for redoing tired seams in teak decks as well as when mending underwater problems. Another somewhat similar product—useful above and below the waterline—is Travaco's Caulk-Tex, a rubberized epoxy that bonds tenaciously to concrete, fiberglass, metal, etc. Two-part versions tend to cure faster and provide a bit more adhesive. Thiokol is the old standby in this category and is used in a two-part product marketed by Boatlife.

Silicone sealers have long been a popular commodity. They tend to be less stiff and flow easily in a wide range of temperatures. Many builders use them to bed hardware, although most tend not to use the product below the waterline. The product sets quickly and is easy to handle. Boatlife, 3M, and Boat Armor market easy-to-use tube and cartridge silicone sealer. 3M's version called T-3 is formulated to work at temperatures up to 600 degrees Fahrenheit, a distinct advantage in some applications.

The third category is polyurethane sealant/adhesives. 3M's #5200 has become a popular item in many boatyards. It is a fine sealer and tenacious adhesive. Boatlife has a variation called Life Seal, which cures quicker and does not harden to the extent of most other polyurethanes. This type of product is useful above, as well as below, the waterline.

These three categories of sealant/adhesive have upstaged conventional lead-based hull and deck seam compounds just as trowel cement has given way to plastic putties. The older products do not perform as well as their new counterparts but may still be found in a few chandleries catering to those who like the smell of oil finishes and tarred marlin.

Teak Treatments

Teak that has become oxidized and is partially covered with dirt and a gummy oil residue must be resurfaced prior to refinishing.

Careful sanding is one alternative. It removes the residue and flattens the raised grain. It also removes a measurable amount of wood. Thin decks with shallow plugs can't be sanded too often or bungs will begin to pop out revealing the underlying screw heads.

Chemical cleaners can often remove oxidized wood without too much effect upon good timber. Eventually, however, the harder areas of lignen in the wood tend to stand proud as softer pulp wood is eroded away. At some point it will be necessary to sand the wood and start from scratch once again.

Teak cleaners vary in their intensity. Single-part powder, such as Teak Brite Cleaner by Boatlife, is a mild abrasive as well as a chemical treatment that softens oxidized areas and allows them to be scrubbed away with a brush. When used in conjunction with plenty of water to flush the surface, a great deal of dirt and residue can be effectively removed. It takes plenty of rinsing to eliminate the powder left behind. More caustic two-part base/acid liquids, such as Travaco's Te-Ka, tend to cut through oxidized wood at a faster pace, but also require attention to detail. If either part *A* or part *B* is left for long periods without being neutralized by the other, discoloration and even paint damage can occur. This is an effective product for those who need to remove serious oxidation in a short amount of time. Attention to detail will pay off.

Other companies such as Knights, Lan-o-Sheen, Flood, etc. also have products available for teak cleaning. I tend to recommend that when a specific manufacturer's teak sealer is chosen, an owner should give the same company's teak cleaners a try. Considerable amounts of research and development work go into the formulation of these products, and it's good to capitalize on such advancements made in the lab.

Solvents, Reducers, Thinners, Cleaners—and More

There was a time when mineral spirits filled the bill for each of these headings. Today the chemistry lab prevails, and the solvents on the shelf are as different as milk and gingerale. The more esoteric the paint, such as polyurethanes and epoxies, the more caustic the solvents. Methyl ethyl ketone, acetone, toluene, and xylol aren't products you want to bathe in or breathe in a small, enclosed place. These volatile solvents are needed to enhance the spraying or brushing behavior of the long-chain polymer paints.

Use the applicator guidelines on the can to determine which solvent is correct for a particular use. Don't use one manufacturer's reducer or solvent with another's product. The quality-control standards could be lower —such as permitting more moisture in xylol. For a few cents, it's not worth taking the chance of voiding a manufacturer's guarantee. Normally the same product can be used to wipe down a hull prior to painting and as a cleaning fluid after the job is completed. All efforts should be made to keep the chemical off the skin. Heavy-duty Playtex dishwashing gloves do a fine job in this category. Easi-Air disposable respirator masks (3M #08540) offer good respiratory protection.

Successful refinishing hinges on the harmony between the paint and the painter. Products are important, but they can only enhance the preparation work that has already been done. When you consider a new material, read all you can about it. Mix up a bit exactly as the manufacturer recommends and apply it to a test patch—on something *not* attached to your boat. When you feel you have things under control, take one last run with the tack rag, check your brush for loose hairs, and always look from the side into the new surface you are laying on.

Ralph Naranjo is a boatyard manager, boat owner, and frequent magazine contributor on the subjects of boat repair and maintenance.

Glossary

Abrasion Resistance How well a surface withstands wearing away by friction. Related to both hardness and toughness.

Abrasive A substance used for wearing away a surface by friction.

Acetone A highly flammable solvent, often used with epoxy and polyester resins and when quick drying is needed. Has a flash point of 14°F.

Acrylic Resins Synthetic resins available in a variety of liquid and solid forms. Solid acrylics include Lucite and Plexiglas.

Adhesion The property which makes a coating or glue bond to a surface.

Air Dry To dry at room temperature: approximately 60 degrees to 80 degrees F with about 50 percent relative humidity.

Alkyds A general descriptive term for synthetic resins of many types. The term is derived from "al" for alcohol and "kyd" for acid, from which alkyds are made.

Alligatoring Refers to a painted surface on which cracks have formed resembling the skin of an alligator. May be caused by application of too thick a coating, among other reasons.

Anhydrous Containing no water, dry.

Antique Finish Usually applied to furniture to give an aged, dappled appearance.

Back Priming A coating applied to the back side of wood to seal it from moisture absorption; often used on plywood.

Batch A quantity of paint or varnish produced in one continuous mixing or blending.

Binder The portion of a paint mixture that holds the pigment particles together.

Bleaching The process of treating wood with an acid or bleach to restore or change the appearance.

Blistering Bubbles on a finished surface caused by heat, grease, moisture in the wood, or anything that causes vapor to form under the coating.

Bloom To sweat or whiten from moisture. Also called blush.

Body A term that describes the consistency (thickness or thinness) of a coating.

Boiled Linseed Raw linseed oil that has been heated (but not boiled) to promote drying. A misnomer.

Bond or Tie Coat   An intermediate coating used to improve adhesion of succeeding coats.

Boxing   Pouring from one container to another as a mixing technique.

Breathable Coating   A coating that has sufficient porosity to expel or admit moisture.

Bridging   When a coating covers a crack or defect in the surface.

Burnishing   Shiny spots on a mat finish caused by rubbing or sweating.

Casein Paint   Derived from milk, usually water thinned.

Catalyst   Something that accelerates a chemical reaction.

Caulk   A slow-drying plastic material used to seal or fill joints.

Cement Finishes   Containing Portland cement. Occasionally used under the waterline on traditional boats.

Chalking   Degradation of paint film, usually evidenced by a powder appearing on the surface.

Checking   Ripples or breaks in the surface of a coating.

Chinawood Oil   Tung oil.

Clouding   Opaque film on a paint or varnish surface. Loss of luster.

Cold-Molded Boat Hulls   A method of construction using thin wood veneer and epoxy as the bonding and sealing agent. Cold-molded hulls are often held together without any mechanical fastenings. Very good weight-to-strength ratios.

Colorfast   A term used to describe a non-fading paint.

Color Retention   The ability to retain color.

Countersink   To pre-drill a hole for a mechanical fastening so that the fastening will be flush with or below the surface. Some fastenings are countersunk far enough to allow the use of a wood plug to seal the hole.

Coverage   The amount of area a coating will cover or hide.

Crawling   A descriptive term for paint or other finish that refuses to adhere to a spot, usually because of grease or oil on the surface.

Crazing   Small interlacing cracks on the surface.

Cutting In   Making a clean, precise edge with a paint brush, such as along a boottop or sheer stripe.

Delamination   Separation of layers, often a result of moisture.

Dew Point   A variable temperature, below which condensation of water begins to occur.

Diatomaceous Earth   A fine abrasive powder consisting of the skeletons of diatoms. Used as flatting agent and for stain removal.

Dry Hard   When a surface has reached its maximum degree of hardness.

Drying Oils   An oil that will dry to a hard surface, as opposed to oils that stay wet. Drying oils usually dry within 48 hours after application.

Dry Rot   A stage of decay when wood can be crushed to a dry powder, usually caused by moisture. A misnomer.

Elasticity   The ability of a coating to flex slightly and return to its original size without breaking.

End Seal Paint, oil, or varnish applied to the ends of boards or end grain to seal from moisture.

Erosion Wearing away of a coating, which exposes the underlying surface.

Exothermic A chemical reaction that gives off heat, such as when epoxy resin is mixed with catalyst.

Fading Loss of color or intensity due to weathering or time.

Feather Edge A tapered edge achieved by sanding or rubbing.

Fillet A web or bead of material, either structural or cosmetic, applied at the junction of two panels or members.

Fisheye A type of cratering in a coating that resembles a fish eye, often with radiating hairline cracks.

Flaking Refers to a condition in which small pieces of a coating lift from the surface.

Flammable Liquid Any liquid that emits flammable vapors below 80°F.

Flash Point The lowest temperature at which a liquid will ignite from spark or flame. An indication of how safe a material may be.

Flat No gloss or luster.

Flatting Agent Any material used in paint or varnish to reduce gloss.

Floor Varnish A type with toughness and durability made just for floors.

Flow The ability of a surface coating to self-level and spread to a consistent film. Coatings that flow well usually do not leave brush marks.

Flow Coating Applying a coating by pouring it onto the surface instead of brushing or spraying it.

Gelcoat A hard, tough, pigmented type of polyester resin used as an exterior surface finish to seal the laminate and provide protection from weathering. Usually applied by spraying to female molds before layup of the fiberglass/polyester resin mix.

Ghosting A term used to describe a coating with an indefinite appearance, with light and dark areas. Incomplete coverage.

Gloss The reflecting ability of a surface.

Gooseflesh Small pimples on a dried coating.

Grain Raising A surface roughness caused by swelling of surface wood fibers.

High Build A coating that produces thick films with each coat.

Holiday Uncoated areas missed during painting or varnishing.

Humidity The amount of water vapor in the atmosphere.

Hydrophilic Water loving; absorbs water.

Hydrophobic Does not absorb water readily.

Hygrometer An instrument used to measure the humidity in the air.

Immiscible A liquid which will not readily mix with another, but separates out forming layers in the container.

Kick To cure, harden.

Laminate A bonding of two or more layers of material, as in plywood or fiberglass.

Lap To extend one coating so that it covers the edge of a previous coating.

Leach To dissolve or dissipate out of a coating.

Long Oil Varnish Has a relatively higher proportion of oil to resin, which makes it tougher and more elastic.

Mat Finish A smooth, even surface without sheen or highlights.

Mechanical Adhesion Depends on surface roughness for an effective bond.

Micron A unit of length equal to 1/100th of a millimeter.

Mildew A fungus-caused discoloration often seen on damp, poorly ventilated surfaces.

Milky Describes a transparent or bright finish that has turned white from moisture.

Mottled Refers to a surface coating that has dried with variations of hue and intensity.

Natural Resins Gums and resins exuded from trees, whether living or fossil.

Non-Drying Oil An oil that will remain tacky, will not dry hard. Examples are castor oil and mineral oil.

Opacity The degree to which a coating will obscure the underlying surface.

Orange Peel A surface condition in which sprayed droplets of paint have not leveled. Resembles the dimpled surface of an orange.

Oxidize To combine with oxygen.

Peeling A condition in which the surface coating separates, sometimes in large pieces. Peeling also describes what happens when a sheathing, such as fiberglass cloth, separates from the surface, due to improper or inadequate sheathing techniques.

Permeability The ability of a vapor or liquid to pass through a coating or membrane. Permeable coatings are not true water seals.

Petroleum Spirits Another name for mineral spirits.

Picking Up Describes the lifting of a coating by paint remover solvents applied over their surface.

Pinholing Tiny holes, sometimes caused by bubbles that remain in a coating as it cures. Sometimes happens to epoxy coatings as a result of being applied in hot sunlight, which does not allow time enough for the catalyzed resin to cure properly, or by agitating the resin too much.

Plank-on-Frame Boat Hulls Traditional type of construction, using keel and ribs as primary members to which fore-and-aft planks are attached with fastenings.

Puddling Laying on of excessive amounts of coating, usually to a flat, level surface. Not recommended except for oil saturation.

Pulling A term used to describe a brush or roller that has started to build up resistance. Usually indicates that thinner is needed.

Raw Oil An oil that has not been treated with heat or chemicals to improve or modify drying characteristics.

Relative Humidity The ratio of the amount of moisture contained in the air to the greatest amount it could hold at that temperature. Measured by a hygrometer.

Retention The ability of a coating to maintain its original colors after exposure to elements and over a period of time.

Ropy Describes a coating when it gets sticky and stringy and will not flow from brush to the surface.

Rottenstone   Similar to pumice stone, used for polishing and abrading. Gives off a distinctive odor.

Sagging   The tendency of a wet coating to flow down a vertical surface, making runs or curtains of uneven thickness.

Sanding Surfacer   A filler material, usually heavily pigmented, intended for building up a surface in preparation to final sanding.

Satin Finish   Sometimes called semi-gloss, or rubbed effect. The finish does not have a full luster.

Scaling   The failure of a coating, usually after moisture has gotten under the surface, causing it to crack. Also called flaking in its severe form.

Self-leveling   Describes a coating that flattens out evenly on a surface, free of "wrinkles," i.e., high spots caused by uneven thickness in the coating or imperfections in the surface.

Settling   The separation of pigments or ingredients when left unstirred. Some coatings must be stirred almost constantly to maintain suspension.

Set Up   To dry hard and firm.

Shadowing   When preceding coatings show through. Similar colors are usually easier to cover, whereas contrasting shades may require additional coats.

Short   A coating is said to be short when it is brittle or when it does not flow easily.

Silica Gel   Used as a drying agent. Capable of absorbing almost 50 percent of its weight in water.

Silicone   A resin made from quartz rock and used as a waterproofing material.

Sinking   A finish is said to be sinking when a large amount of it is absorbed by the surface.

Size or Sizing Agent   A sealing coat, usually a thick coating applied to a porous surface to prepare for subsequent coatings.

Skippy   When paint is too heavy-bodied to flow properly, leaving some spots too heavily coated and others too thin.

Slip   The opposite of pull. A term used to describe the brushability of a coating.

Solvents   A term usually applied to paint additives that evaporate during drying. Used to modify consistency to aid application, or to help in cleanup.

Spot Priming   Priming or painting of specific localized spots.

Stiff   Describes a coating that is hard to control with a brush and needs thinning.

Stippled Finish   A finish produced by dabbing or poking the bristle ends of a brush onto a surface. Produces a rougher surface. Sometimes used to apply extra coating in one area to seal a surface.

Surface Drying   Describes a condition in which a coating skins over but stays wet underneath.

Tack Free   When a surface can be touched without sticking; also when dust will no longer stick.

Tooth   The degree of roughness needed to provide a good mechanical bond on a sanded surface.

Topsides   A term usually used to describe the hull sides above the waterline and below the deck. Sometimes refers to all surfaces on a boat above the waterline.

TSP Trisodium phosphate. A bleaching solution available in powder form at marine and paint stores.

Viscosity A resistance to flow, modified by thinners, solvents, driers, and thickeners.

Wet-Sanding A method of sanding by flooding the surface to be sanded with water or oil and then sanding with special water-resistant sandpaper. Wet sanding lubricates the surface while carrying away dust and other effluents; it usually produces a very fine surface.

Wicking Capillary action, which draws or absorbs liquid.

Wow An imperfection or unevenness in a surface.

Index